Based on a True Story

BEHIND THE SCENES

Pamela Marshall

Written by:
Pamela Marshall
pamelamarshall69@gmail.com

Edited by:
April Smiley

BEHIND THE SCENES

MOCY PUBLISHING
WWW.MOCYPUBLISHING.COM

Detroit, Michigan

BEHIND THE SCENES

ISBN 978-0-9834700-9-0
Copyright © 2013 by Pamela Marshall

Published by Mocy Publishing, LLC.
Website: www.mocypublishing.com
Email: info@mocypublishing.com
Phone: (313) 436-6944

All rights reserved. Except as permitted under the United States Copyright Act of 1976, no part of this publication may be reproduced or distributed in any form or by any means, or stored in a data base or retrieval system, without the prior written permission of the publisher.

Acknowledgements

I chose phases to show the progress of my life in this book. Keeping it direct and honest about my life, I had no chapters in my experiences and none in the telling.

I would like to acknowledge the following people. My cousin Shamise King, who challenged me to write my story. Special thanks to Karen hopes who has never given up on me through my many struggles, remains to be my true friend and sponsor. I also like to give a special thanks to Margaret Adams-Smith for continuing to push me, knowing my setbacks and inspiring me to come back and reach greater heights.

To my dear friends for believing that I could write this book, Chris Majors, my mentor whom I have watched achieve success.

Introductions

I met this girl when I was 14 she was everything I wasn't, she had a fearless mind, she was determined to win at all cost, she had fierce force that couldn't be tamed, she had hands of a magician, she could con herself into anything and out of everything, she could charm a snake, it took me a long time to figure out why she wanted to be my friend, she kept me in trouble, she didn't have children, but I did, she had no family, but I did, she could do anything she wanted without consequences, I always took the rap, it became clear she became my friend to kill me, she knew I was weak and I hid behind her, she had the guts and spunk I didn't have, she made my mind black, she made my body sick, she wouldn't feed me and she beat me every day, she made me sleep with dirty men and women, she made me burn bridges until they were irreparable, she told me you will prey on the elderly, you will destroy marriages, you will laugh at disaster, I will send you to jail to rest for the next caper, she made me walk away from my very own children, every time I would get a positive friend, here she comes to be good to me for a while, only to pull me away from the good, she hated healthy relationships, she kept me from GOD, school, and anything positive to help me only to leave me when I got into trouble. She told me one day while I slept, "I will kill you if it's the last thing I do, there will be no chance of survival, you will kill, you will destroy, you will be my hoe, and I will always come back if you try to leave me, you are nothing without me, I made you, I help you stand and don't ever forget it". When I woke up, I cried till my eyes were swollen shut, I was lonely and had nowhere to go, I battled with her for twenty three years, I heard about JESUS but I didn't know him, I prayed, suddenly I got my own balls and sat down and premeditated a real murder, and with malice and forethought, I killed her, I was jailed. When I became free, there was a new me, a beautiful lady with class, a strong mind and body, I was spared once more. Dedicated to the girl I once knew Jean.

Phase One

It's the summer of 1983. I'm on the corner of Puritan and Hamilton in Highland Park, a small city inside of Detroit, Michigan. I was standing there lost, exhausted, scared, and on my own with no direction and no money. I was a fugitive from a girls home. Everything that was going on around me, the traffic zooming by, people walking about, was like music to my ears because I was free. The only sounds for months were of other little girls crying for their parents to get them out of there. I was abandoned. I was picked up and dropped off into a world that no little girl could ever be prepared for. As I stood on Puritan Street, my thoughts were on what happened in my past life that brought me to this point.

My life was something you can't imagine. I was lonely, living in this big ass house with these people I didn't know. Talk about being lost. We went from a loving home with my grandmother to living with my uncle David Johnson, who was a preacher at Hope Baptist church. Uncle David was so sweet, but his wife was doing what most wives do, just following suit. There was no real love from her. You could detect she was a fake. Well, to me anyway.

My thoughts even as a child were I don't like these people. I could feel they didn't like us either, me or my little brother. The Johnson's, man…their family is known all over the world, but if you really knew them back then, they were just as fucked up as we were. This all happened to me when I was eight years old. At that age I spoke my mind, yet silenced myself when I was locked away in a home. The preacher's wife got rid of me and kept my brother.

Nobody wanted me, not even my dead mother's rotten, selfish, holier than thou, sisters. They were all full of shit, except one who took in my oldest sister, my aunt, Sherrie Fontaine. My aunts were all in the position to take care of us, yet instead, they allowed us to be separated and shipped around to where we didn't know each other. Even to this day we don't know each other. Aunt Sherrie had her special pick which I found out later. They were just rotten as far as I was concerned. If something were to happen to my sister, I would be there for her children. I would help my niece or nephew.

Suddenly I was startled out of my deep thoughts with the sound of loud music. BOOM BA BOOM! I snapped out my trance hearing this excessively loud, ear shattering music. The music was coming from an approaching car. My appearance to this NIGGA who drove up was that I was old enough for whatever and anything. My hips had curves and my butt was just the right size. My face had cleared up from a horrible case of acne. My braces, which I had worn for five years, were off. I had inherited my mother's fine hair that lay in the center of my back. My eyes were dark brown and they were slanted. Most people said I was pretty, but I really didn't think so.

Anyway, the driver of the car said, "Hey little lady you are so pretty. Where are you going?" I said, "I'm looking for a store", shyly because this wasn't a boy he was a man. He asked where I was from and told me there wasn't a store around there. He offered me a ride. He was cool but he wasn't cute like Billy Doyle and Gary Cox, boys I had a crush on from middle school.

He opened the door and I jumped in, which was my first mistake. This man was huge like a body builder. He was tall, he had a long scar across his nose, and one of his teeth was missing on the left side of his mouth. He was wearing a hat tilted to the side with a serious lean that made me think he was a pimp. He was dressed really sharp in one of those fancy jogging suits. I felt like a big girl, so I acted like one. He asked, "What's your name?" I told him my name was Pam. He said "You don't look like a Pam. You look like sunshine. Who do you live with?" I told him the truth, I didn't live anywhere. I just ran away from Vista Maria, a girls home. He was shocked. I could tell he was putting something together in his mind. He was quiet and deep in thought, like he was pondering over something as he pulled into the store parking lot.

He was scaring me. He was looking at me hard, as if he could see through me. Then he asked, " How old are you Sunshine?" I told the truth again. I was fourteen. He just turned his head and got out of the car. I just sat there. I felt lonelier than I did on the corner he got me from. He leaned over the sunroof and asked, "Whatcha want out the store Sunshine?" I asked for some cigarettes. I had picked the smoking habit up from some of the girls in the home. He smiled, shook his head, and walked away.

He left the keys in the ignition and "Easy" by the Commodores was playing on the radio. The sun was out and the other girls were still at Vista. Me, I was free, free of pain. I was thinking about how much I missed my Grandma Lee. When she died that's when I went bad. I hated that she was gone. She was my life. I was daydreaming and when I looked up, I saw that he was coming back to the car. I tried to look mature but I felt really stupid. I always daydreamed, especially when I was a little girl. I don't remember having any neighborhood friends to talk to.

Anyway, as he was coming to the car, I noticed this bulge in his pants. It was big and I got a little uncomfortable watching it. I had never been alone with a man before, especially a stranger. I had nobody to call and nowhere to go. My hope was that this man would help me, but he just smacked the bottom of the Kool cigarette package and handed me a lit cigarette. I thought to myself, this is it. I knew then he was the man that was going to show me something I never saw before. And guess what? He did.

He looked over at me to watch me smoke. I guess to see if I could. I asked him why he was looking at me. He smiled and said, "Here we go." He turned up the music and pulled out of the parking lot. The sun was setting. It was a pretty evening. He asked, "Do you want to ride?" I grabbed his extended hand and said, "Let's ride." I didn't know it was going to be the ride of my life.

I had never been in the front seat of a car. I felt like a woman, smoking cigarettes and drinking

Bartles and Jaymes coolers on a hot sunny day. We didn't talk for awhile. I guess we were both thinking about where this encounter would lead. He was so much older than me. He could pass for my dad. We headed Downtown. The city looked so big to me. I was born and raised in Detroit, and had never really been anywhere in my own city. This was definitely new and exciting. I felt like I was in another world. He was kind to me. The way he spoke was mild and warm. He offered to buy me everything I needed. I didn't bring any of my things from the home. He seemed to be in deep thought.

I was thinking too. What do I do now? Is this guy going to kill me? Every girl has that thought, especially, if you placed yourself in harms way by jumping in a car with a total stranger. Anyway, he drove down Jefferson. We were headed to Belle Isle Park. I knew how to get there because of our church picnics.

As we were riding, I thought about my Uncle David. He made life look easy. When he was around, everything was all right. He made little jokes to make me laugh. He was very kind to me. He always dressed sharp and smelled good. When my Grandmother was on her death bed, she asked him to keep me and my brother.

We were the lost children. My mother's name was Rose and she was a beautiful black woman who had four children. It was my sister, my two brothers, and me. She was a heroin addict who got caught up in the life of drugs. She was murdered while in the game. Two weeks before her death, my mom dropped us off at the police station. From there we were sent to the D J Healy Home for Children. It was 1972. At that time my mother couldn't keep us. The drugs were more powerful than she thought. She loved us enough to give us away instead of abusing us further.

My Grandmother, who we called Gramps, kept me and my little brother. My sister was with my aunt, Mrs. Fontaine. I don't remember who had my eldest brother. I know it had to be rough for my mother back then, because they would put you in jail for getting high. My Gramps always said that I was the identical replica of my mother all the way from my slanted eyes to the bottom of my feet. When Gramps got sick and passed away, so did I. A part of me died when my Gramps passed. She was the last real connection to my mom. There wasn't anyone else who could tell me anything about her.

The car hit a bump and I snapped out of my daydream. I did that a lot. I looked up we were crossing the bridge to Belle Isle. As we drove over the Detroit River, I asked, "Can I stick my head out of the sunroof?" "Go ahead", he said. He pushed a button, the sunroof rolled back and it was the sweetest thing ever. I stood on the seat and he pushed me up from my butt. It was the first time anybody had ever touched me on my butt other than my grandmother's spankings. I was free. My hair blew in the wind. My arms were out wide and my smile was big as the sky. I laughed loud. He drove slowly so I could enjoy the moment. There was a curve ahead. He tapped my leg to indicate for me to slide down. I smiled and he smiled too. He was not cute but he was harmless enough, so I thought.

I had no business with this man. I should have stayed in the home but I couldn't live like that anymore. I'd moved so many places while I was young. I was tired. I just wanted to belong to someone. But that can come with a hell of a price.

He pulled over to the side. He looked at me with a serious look and said, "Tell me." "Tell you what", I asked him. Then I said, "Tell me your name." He must of thought he told me his name, he said, "Oh yeah, it's Jay." He asked me what happened and why was I in a girl's home. I always told the truth about myself, so I began to tell him how I was sent to live with this family that didn't love me or my brother. They had seven children and they were funny acting towards me and my brother. I also was gutsy, rebellious, and very hard headed because I wouldn't listen to them. I had just been told my Gramps was never coming back so my attitude was not pleasant at all. It was actually unbearable.

My brother on the other hand was a mild mannered child. He was very adorable and everyone liked him. He was very cute, a good kid, and he followed suit. Me, I knew I wouldn't last there long. They made us go to church. It seemed like we went every day. We lived in a mansion that was so huge our back yard looked like a golf course. We could only go so far into the yard. I knew these people weren't our family for real. I didn't feel loved. I never did as far as I can remember. I knew something was missing. I daydreamed a lot back then. Mainly about who was my real mother and what really happened to us. Why did we have to live with these people and most importantly how to get away?

I had planned a getaway scheme but before I could put it in motion that bitch, the preacher's wife, sent me away. She treated me differently than my brother and I knew she didn't like me. The woman never even hugged me. Her so called love was given begrudgingly, and that hurt me as a child. When you're a kid, you have feelings and you can tell when an adult doesn't care for you. People don't realize that if you're mistreated as a kid it has a lot to do with how you grow.

One sunny afternoon a very pretty lady in a grey dress took me away from the Johnson's. This woman took me to Vista Maria. That place looked like hell. The walls looked like they could breathe and swallow you up. There were brick walls painted grey and the rooms were small, not fun for a small child. The place looked really scary. You knew you weren't at home because there wasn't any love there either.

I was bullied by the other girls. For some reason, I always stood out from the rest of the crowd. I was always targeted for chaos. I got beat up a lot and felt punished for being born.

One night I couldn't sleep, my friend came to me and said, "Bitch get up". Now my friend has always been a part of my life and we would talk all the time. She said, "You see that window over there? Go check it out. We have to get out of here!" She said it harshly. It seemed that she's always spoken to me like that, aggressive and rude. The night guard was entering the lot. My friend told me, "He leaves at 9 a.m. and so do we."

I was scared but she said, "Don't be scared." I trusted her, so I stopped being scared and did what she told me to do for us to be free. After I checked out the window, I laid back down and drifted back to sleep. She came back whispering to me, "Get up Pam. Come on and get up! It's 8:30!" I jumped up and grabbed my things. She said, "Leave them. It'll only slow us down." I listened to her because she was strong. She was completely fearless ever since I've known her.

We crept down the back stairs and entered the employee's parking lot. We found the guard's car, a Ford pickup truck with a bunch of garbage in the back. We didn't care about the garbage. We jumped in and hid under it. We had to get through that gate. The ride to the gate seemed like it took forever. My heart was racing and I was crying as usual. I also cried a lot growing up. My friend said, "Bitch shut up! You will make it. I will always be here to protect you."

In the distance, I heard Mr. Kincaid open the guard shack door as he was changing shift. He was talking to the relief guard Ms. Davis. I wasn't at Vista long but Jean did a lot of listening and calculating. That's how we knew their names. The guards were not affiliated with the children. They had a job to do and that was to watch the grounds.

I was uncomfortable. I had to pee and the garbage smelled really bad. My friend told me to cool out and stay focused. Mr. Kincaid opened his truck door and started it up. We started moving and my heart started beating faster. The ride seemed to last a life time. He made a turn. I knew we were going to stop somewhere. We had been riding for a while. When he turned the truck off, I took a look, jumped up, and got out the truck. We were at a gas station on Schaefer Street near Michigan Avenue in Dearborn, just outside of Detroit.

I still had to pee, so I ducked behind the bushes in someone's yard. I walked until I ended up in Highland Park. Jay had a strange look on his face when I told him this. He asked, "Where is your friend now?" I told him, "She's still around. She only comes when I need her or when she wants me to do stuff." "So, you're alone living in the street?" he asked. I replied, "YUP!" He was quiet for awhile and just looked out the windshield. Then he said, "I'll take care of you, I'm calling you Sunshine. No one needs to know your name."

He was twenty five years old, and he became my savior. He bought me clothes. He fed me, and he gave me money. He took me to a house on Pasadena in Highland Park. I thought this man was everything. He was funny and exciting. He showed me love, but it was a different love. I had felt love before from my Gramps. I thought when people bought you things and fed you it was a form of love. I never once thought he had an ulterior motive. When we got to the house, it was time for me to pay up. I had no idea that he was going to be my man. I had never had one. I never had a boyfriend. I was the preacher's kid. We couldn't talk to boys. It was unheard of.

A lot of people were at the house on Pasadena. I'd never been around that many men before, except in church. They were drinking and smoking funny smelling cigarettes. The men smelled funny too. They seemed to be happy, talking loud, laughing, playing horse shoes, and some were playing cards. He introduced me to them as Shine. Their names were Bo, T-Ball and Q. They had turned the basement into a freak fun house. People were coming and going. Some got kicked out and cussed out. It was funny and sad. I had never seen one man control many men. Jay had power. It was a scary place, but my friend loved it there. She said, "Girl this is it! All grown-ups and no kids. I got you. We'll be all right." She could sense my fear. She always could.

I took a deep breath and relaxed. Jay went to the top of the stairs and said, "I will be busy for awhile." That meant don't bother him. I didn't know I was his business. It had been almost five hours since I met him and I had a home, clothes, and a daddy. I didn't know he wanted to fuck me. I heard about fucking from the girls at Vista. A lot of them were already doing it. NOT ME!!!! I was the preacher's step child, so sex just wasn't it for me. I never thought about it.

When we reached his room my heart started beating faster and I felt like running but my feet were bolted to the floor I couldn't run or walk. I was in a trance. Then my friend popped up in a nick of time. "HEY!!! MOVE BITCH! Move your feet. This will be easy. Just give it up. And you will get served. Once he gets you, he will love it and you will to after awhile. I'll show you how to fuck this ugly but nice NIGGA."

He asked if I was alright. My friend did all the talking. Her name is Jean. Jean was so much stronger than me and she could handle anything. She spoke up quick, "I'm fine. Can I call you daddy?" With a grin on his face he said, Hell yeah!" He pushed open the door. WOW! I was amazed. I thought I was in heaven. I didn't know I was in hell. There was a big bed in the middle of the room. He had a bunch of expensive stuff. He had a lot of clothes and many pairs of gym shoes, not one pair of church shoes.

    There were pictures all around the walls of him and people that looked like movie stars. They were all dressed up. Some had on flashy jewelry. Some were younger looking and some were older cats. Some held sparkly cups and some wore capes.
    I knew what pimps looked like from when we were allowed to watch TV at the Johnsons house. Everyone on the pictures had money, including Jay. I felt so lucky.

    But then my body went numb when he took off his clothes. He acted like I knew what to do. I honestly didn't. Jean said, "I'll show you this one time how to fuck this ugly but nice NIGGA. And let him teach you what he likes." I wanted to cry I had never had sex before. OH MY GOD!!!!!!!!! His penis was huge. I was shocked. I had only seen my little brothers and that was when we stayed with Gramps and took baths together. He told me to come to him.

It was like I completely changed. I transformed. I walked over to him with fear in my eyes and worry on my face. He promised not to hurt me. He said, "Let's rest." He popped a scary movie in the VCR. We laid there together. I remember him rubbing my hair until I fell asleep.

I was exhausted from the long walk after jumping out of the guard's truck. When I woke up I couldn't talk. Jean was moaning. Jay was sucking on me. My lil pussy had never been touched. I rose up to watch. I wanted to see what was happening. My body started doing things I couldn't explain. It felt strange, but good. Then this strong huge black ugly man was on me, then in me. A tear dropped from one eye.

I began to push him off me. It hurt, and felt kind of good. I wanted the hurt to stop, so I kept trying to push him away. He looked down at me and kept fucking me. He then he thrust in me real hard. He started to shake and holler loud, strange noises I never heard before. Then with his salty sweat and heavy weight, he laid on me breathing really hard. He was finished and I was so glad.

Jean looked at me and said, "See you can do it. I will show you how to put it in the back of your mind. You will be fine. Trust me." I trusted her. I remember him rolling off me and snoring like a savage beast immediately. I was in shock. I just laid there for awhile. My legs hurt and my body throbbed. I stayed there frozen until I went to sleep. Morning came quickly and so did my lessons. He began to teach me things about the streets and the people of them. He taught me how to survive by any means. Jay continued to sex me, teach me, feed me, dress me, and he spoiled me.

I really didn't like him. I appreciated him for helping me, but Jean loved him. She had her reasons. I would find out later. She loved his ways so much. She thought everything he did was awesome. It was like he was a GOD or something. But Jean was my girl, my friend, so I had to listen to her. She knew how to handle everything and take away the pain. I had a lot of deep rooted issues and hidden pain only she and I knew about. She was so strong and everything she said and did seemed right. She told me things that would make me feel comfortable with this man even though sometimes I felt like it was wrong and tried to question what I was doing.

I became this star everyone knew as Jay's girl. When you are the dope man's girl, you're somebody. I was his baby. I had no idea I was a project to him. My lessons were learned the hard way. I had absolutely no real family. He was all I had. I watched him every day of the month. I had never seen so much money or so much violence. Everything came like first nature to him. To me, it was like watching TV, but real. There was a long mirror at the bottom of the steps. I looked in it all the time, me and Jean. Jean had dark eyes and long hair like me. We were built the same. When Jean looked in the mirror, she glared at herself. It was kind of ghastly, like she had power. She didn't have low self esteem, but I did. Her life was fun. She was so wild. She did everything to the extreme and I mean everything.

When I looked in the mirror, I second guessed everything from how my hair looked to if my head was too big. I looked more at my flaws than at my beauty. I made sure my clothes fit right. I never wore sandals, heels or pumps. I wore gym shoes, Adidas track suits, and short sets. Jay kept me in cute clothes and a bunch of jewelry. Jean wore stuff that made her look like a whore. She didn't care. I wanted to play with dolls and go to school. But she wanted to play devil street games. When I turned to the side to see my body, I was startled by Jean. She came around in ways I could not believe or explain. She was like a ghost popping in and out. I couldn't understand where she came from and how she got in, but she did. No one ever saw her.

We talked every time she came around. She said, "I heard your daddy talking. He needs to send you to a friend of his to get some money." Why would he need money? He's got his own I thought. Jean said, "You will get this man's money for him." It was the first time I had heard of this friend. I said, "Jean you do it, I don't want to hurt anyone."

As time went by, I heard about things my daddy did. I didn't want to be a part of them. Jean said, "You won't hurt him, you'll just do him like you do your daddy. You're going to fuck him." I started crying. Jean slapped my face hard and said, "Snap out of it. You will get this man's money. Now put this on." She handed me a skirt and heels. "Take off those gym shoes and work it bitch!!!" she yelled at me. I slowly nodded as if I was programmed. I changed my clothes. My daddy came down the stairs. He said, "Now that's my baby. I will buy you anything you want. It won't take long. I need you to concentrate."

I didn't understand that my job was to fuck a stranger and rob him. I couldn't do it. On the drive to the Crown motel on Woodward Avenue, I felt ugly and bad. Jean was in the back seat. She said, "I can't stand your whimpering. Slide over. I'll do it!" When daddy stopped on the corner, we both got out. He handed me the key to room six. The man was already in the room. My job was to get his pants and run out. It didn't go smooth. It was all fucked up. I walked to the ground level room looked up at the door. The number 6 was the spot. I turned the key in the lock, took a deep breath, and went in.

An elderly man was seated in a chair by the table. He looked like one of the deacons at my uncle's church. He had salt and pepper hair, even in his beard. He looked like a black Santa. He was fat and cheery. He spoke, "Hey there little lady." He had a smirk on his face. He must have had to spend a lot of money for my daddy to send me to him. Jean did all the talking, "Hey big daddy." She ran to his side and hugged and kissed him. She was rubbing his back and stripping him of his clothes, nice and slow. "What can I do for you?" she asked. With those cold black eyes and perfect white teeth, she looked like a pretty devil.

He was all over her young and flawless body. I was in shock. Jay was my first and now he's passing me to different men. I thought he loved me. Wow! What kind of shit is this? The man smelled of liquor and cigars. He was sweaty. Jean wasn't weak. She started sucking his chest and got down to his penis. She said, "You're sweaty daddy. Let's take a shower." She stripped quickly and started the shower. He placed his pants so that whatever was in there wouldn't fall out. I watched. I was scared. They went into the bathroom together.

Jean came right out and went into his pants and gave the money to me. Before she could get back to Santa, someone entered the room. It wasn't room service either. It was a middle aged woman with a big black gun in her hand. She had tears streaming down her face. She looked tired and her eyes were blood shot red as if she had been drinking. Jean left. She was gone. It was just me with all this man's money in my panties. I started peeing on myself. The woman said, "Who are you? Put your clothes on and where is he?" She said everything fast and back to back. I was petrified. I couldn't move. I never had a gun pointed at me, let alone seen one. She said, "Who the fuck are you? I will not ask again." I whispered, "My name is Sunshine. I was sent here to fuck him. He never told me he had a wife."

I could tell she was his wife. She had a huge diamond on her finger. She was crying hysterically. I thought she was going to shoot me. Urine started running down my legs as I tried to finish getting dressed. She asked me how old was I. I told her 14. She told me to get out. Now Santa never came back out the bathroom. There was only one way in and one way out. All I know is I was scared, half naked, and leaving room 6. But I had the money. At least my daddy wouldn't be mad. Where the hell did Jean go? I started running as fast as I could half dressed.

I felt kind of bad for Santa. Before I reached the corner, my daddy was in position. The door was open and the car running. I heard the shot when I was closing the door. BAM!!!!!!!!!!! It sounded like a cannon. Tears burned my eyes and I couldn't see. I reached in my panties and handed my daddy the money. He smiled and rubbed my head. "What's wrong Sunshine? You did good girl."

I knew she killed her husband. She had to be following him. Yet she spared my life. She knew I was young and didn't know any better. Jay seemed not to have any feelings. I knew he heard the shot. I just stared at him. It was the first and last time I felt sorry for someone. He made sure of that.

"What's wrong with you?" he asked. I couldn't speak. I was saturated with my own urine. I was not only scared shitless, I was in shock. If it wasn't for Jean, I wouldn't have made it. But why did she leave? Jay shouted, "What the fuck is wrong with you?" I replied softly, "Nothing. I just want to go home." He lifted my head and saw my tears and held my face tight. He was still driving. It was the first time I saw someone drive with their knee. He controlled everything, my emotions, and my fear.

Then he showed me how not to feel. The car was steady and his eyes were locked on mine. He said "If I see fear again, make sure it's from me kicking your ass. People don't give a damn about you, so stop caring about them. You will earn your keep but I will help take care of you." I felt trapped in a situation that scared me but I wasn't sure if I wanted to get out of it.

Phase One taught me how to be a heartless bitch.

Phase Two

A year had passed by. It became easy to do the work asked of me. Jean had completely taken over. She ran my life for me. I had fallen in love with Jay. Sex became easier, in fact I loved it. I wanted to give him a child so we never wore a condom. But I never got pregnant. I thought something was wrong with me. Nothing was wrong. It wasn't meant to be. I started getting a grown woman's body after my 15th birthday.

I looked good and flawless on the outside but I was dirty as hell on the inside. It's easy to clean up the outside but how do you clean the inside? I always felt dirty. My outward appearance was perfect but my heart was broken. My spirit was filthy, not to mention my soul. I really didn't think I had one. I was a mess, even at fifteen.

Jean thought it best I wear make up from time to time. I had boyish ways. I wanted to be just like my daddy Jay. I watched him with an eagle eye. It became clear that my GOD was Jay. I leaned on his every word. My prayers were few. They became prayers that asked please let me get away with this, instead of Jesus help me. When the jobs got bigger, it was time for me to learn how to drive. Sometimes the jobs were for Jay and his buddies. I did what was asked of me, whatever it was. When I made mistakes, I would get my ass beat. But being with him was a must. I needed this man in ways I couldn't understand. I loved him more than I loved myself.

As soon as fall arrived he put me in school. I had been kicked out of Detroit public schools for the unthinkable. I had a few words with a girl named Stacey McMillan that led to a disagreement. I set her hair on fire. She had a Jeri curl. I could have killed this girl and I wanted to. A lot of my behavior was not of the average teenager.

I had a severe issue with mama jokes. It's still a touchy subject for me today. Whatever she said wasn't funny. It was worth her head, literally. Jean was vicious from day one. I remember she threw my brother David down a flight of stairs for fun. I was seven at the time. I asked my brother if he wanted to play ghost and he said yes. I pulled one of my grandmother's good sheets out the linen closet. I placed it over his head and guided him through each room upstairs to play this vicious game. I took him to the top of the stairs and violently threw him down the stairs to his possible death. What child plays that way?

I remember she bullied me into making my brother jump from the roof of a garage onto a cherry tree. I knew full well he was scared and he would hurt his self. He did. He was such a wimp to her. I forced him to do it and when he did, he knocked himself out. He never made it to the tree. He hit the tree and slid down and hit the concrete. He was knocked out for a long time with cherry juice all over his face and head. I thought it was blood. All the other children left. I couldn't even go home without him. I thought he was dead. I was scared and cried a lot. Then he woke up. He jumped up so fast immediately hollering. I was so glad he was alive.

I knew we were late for dinner. My grandmother was going to get in my hide as usual. It seemed like devilment was a part of my life from the very beginning. Looking back, I learned that Jean was mean even then. She started planting her seeds while I was young. I think to myself that Ted Bundy was a child once also.

I was in school before I ran away from the home. Jay figured if he wanted to keep me, I had to be enrolled in a school. Back then any adult could enroll you in school. It didn't have to be your parent. But in reality, he was my parent. He enrolled me in Highland Park High. I felt lost in school. I didn't fit in. I day dreamed a lot and Jean's constant nagging to skip didn't help either. Plus my classmates got on my nerves with their petty problems about what to wear to school each day and who was the cutest boy in school. I was already grown. No one knew what I did for a living. I had already lived a life unknown to most these kids. My teachers were like stick people. They were there but I wasn't focused. Jean didn't like this big place with no windows. She looked at it like it was a jail.

She told me she had better things for us to do. We went shopping. I was already skilled at stealing. This job was much more fun than school. I was able to get my man some things plus Jean seemed to need an outfit every day. At first it was a few days a week, school then shopping. Then it became hustling, no school. I stayed mad at Jean. She always disappeared when I got caught. She had balls of steel. She could do anything and wouldn't flinch or cry. Jean was evil and she loved being deviant.

On June 1st my man went to jail for selling drugs. I was completely devastated. It became a time of chaos. I had no guidance. I had no one to tell me what to do or how to do it. I felt things. I knew when bad things were going to happen. I just had a feeling when he didn't show to pick me up from school that something had happened. I had to walk home. Now that wasn't good at all. I was use to riding or driving myself. I always had jealous people to deal with. It was my looks, the way I dressed, or flat out just being myself posting a problem.

There was a girl who had jumped me with her brother one day. Jay pistol whipped them for it. Now that he was gone, it was her time to get even. The word was out that my man was one of the biggest dealers in Highland Park so nobody fucked with me. But this time my daddy wasn't there.

My daddy taught me how to fight. He would make me fight him back. After a surprise sucker punch here and there, I had no fear of anyone hitting me, especially a kid. This bitch Shanay took the liberty of trying once more to jump me after school. Now my man is gone and Jean is nowhere around. This dumb bitch wanted some physical bruising.

My daddy taught me that while one is approaching take that time to measure your distance. Keeping them off me was a must at all times. But no one could hit me as hard as he did. Fear wasn't an option. Shanay walked up to me and said, "I got you now you buck tooth bitch. Where is your man and his fancy car now?" As she got closer my hands started tingling and I had to pee. Neither of us knew I was going to beat this bitch to a pulp.

I always carried a weapon. I reached in my pocket and grabbed a cue ball that was in one of Jay's sweat sox. I had no idea she would bleed like she did and loose teeth like a small child. Well they fell out after the first blow. Because my daddy talked when he hit me, I talked when I hit her. I said, "All you bitches will raise up off me." It was the last time I had ever seen or been in a classroom. I never went back to school and Shanay never looked the same.

Then Jean showed up. She laughed at me and said, "It's about time bitch." She was happy that I stood up for myself. I always needed help from her in that area. You would have thought someone was killed the way we ran from the school. The kids looked on with fear and shock. I had become a monster with no conscience. We made it home. I wasn't worried about the police. No one knew where I lived. I started wondering if Shanay was okay. Jean slapped my face hard and screamed, "Bitch, do you think she would have worried about you? From this day forward no remorse. Say it!" I said it but I didn't mean it.

I was scared of Jean. She was a tough pill to swallow at times. She didn't give a shit about any one, not even me. When we reached Pasadena there were no cars, no guys, no drugs, and no guns. The house was completely shut down. Mother Sadie was the only one there. She was Jay's stepmother. She told me that my daddy was sending someone for me. I needed to pack some things and be ready. She didn't have any more information and didn't go into what happened either. As we waited, I didn't give a second thought about the events of the day. I just wanted my man.

A little blue Mustang pulled up. I never saw this lady before. She was pretty. She looked like a real Indian with deep dimples in her cheeks. Her name was Lachelle. She had a pretty smile, overly friendly. But she was doing what she was told to do by Jay. He was already going back and forth to court about some things I knew nothing about. He was sent away for a year. He sent Lachelle to take care of me.

I remember him telling me it would be a time when I would be on my own and how I had to protect myself from people like him. I didn't understand it then, surely I do now. I felt like I lost my blood. I was weak. I didn't have sex from him, money from him, no instructions, no fighting, nothing. All I had was this dumb bitch he sent to watch out for me while he was away in jail.

The moment he was arrested I felt the loss. He was gone. Nothing was funny. I couldn't eat. I was without a soul already. I was a walking shell. I felt every inch of my depression. As she drove her Mustang, I looked at her eyes, her ears, her hands, and every detail of her body. Jean was attracted to her, for many reasons. She always had a motive. She checked her insurance papers when she got out the car. Lachelle ran errands for my daddy, making pickups and drop offs. Of course, I hit her stash every time she got out the car. I was on the grind. See I didn't have my daddy and all I'm told is to roll with this bitch. As always I followed the rules. That shit was about to change.

Jean had full control of the situation now and there was no middle man. My daddy was in jail. The last time Lachelle got out the car Jean said, "Hi cutie." She rarely talked nice to me. I smiled and zeroed in. Our talks were far and few in between unless she really needed me. I watched this bitch go into the places I was never allowed. Jean tapped me on my shoulder. "Snap out of it. I'm talking to you." I looked in the mirror. She was right there.

She began to soothe me about my decision making seeing how it was always fucked up. She said, "Pam I love you. I need you to survive while you're in these streets. That's why I'm so hard on you. You will not ever fail to complete a task." The tears started to well up, she said "No. No. No. You stay strong. I need for you to stay strong. I can't live without your strength, that's why I leave when things go wrong I can't handle failure."

I looked in the mirror again. I told Jean that I am lost when she leaves me. She gives me the character and strength to make it each day. I told Jean I was going to be sixteen soon. I knew it wouldn't be a sweet sixteen. I have never had a birthday party. I needed her with me to help make the best out of it. Jean said, "You don't need anybody but me. Don't trust this bitch right off. We can use her for as long as your daddy is away. You'll have a sweet sixteen it will just be different." Jean tapped into a part of my mind I tried to stay away from as much as possible.

She said "I know you're sad about your mom's murder. But that's what you get when you're weak. She got killed because she didn't kill that bitch first. See I didn't want to tell you this, but I've been around a long time Pam. I used to be your mom's friend too. That's how I knew about you. She died so young. That's why I'm still fit. She was really a weak person. I had to stay off to the side and watch her walk into her own death."

I asked Jean what was my mother like she told me, "She was beautiful. You look just like her and you act like her too. You laugh like her. You're identical in everything you do. She made a man her savior too. Except that heroin was a no-no and she couldn't live without it. I can say she loved you. You were her special child. You were different out of the four." I was a trick baby and the rest of my brothers and sister shared the same father.

Jean knew everything. She filled me with wisdom that was untouchable. I believed her. She was so real to me and down to earth. I couldn't figure out how she was around to know my mom though until many years later. But it didn't matter, my mom's long gone she can't help me now. Suddenly Jean said, "Here she comes. Now I want you to watch this bitch. Ask her about her plans for you. We'll talk later. I'll rest and prepare for your birthday." I still did not know it was my funeral she was preparing me for. Lachelle got in the car and said, "A penny for your thoughts." I would never tell about my relationship with Jean. She told me no one can ever know. I didn't respond to her question. I kept staring out the window.

I was hungry. We went to McDonald's and she gave me graphic details about her plan for me. I still had to remember my lessons and the first one was if you give them nothing they got nothing. So I didn't talk much about me. I just listened and processed it all for Jean. I asked her all kinds of questions and this bitch told me all her business. Where she lived, how she made money, who her family was and such, and how she was related to my daddy.

Wow! Maybe she didn't have to ask much. She may have already known my status, which made me watch her intently with the eagle eye as I call it. See an eagle can see his prey on the ground from the tallest mountain in the world. That's how I was able to see through people. I learned at an early age the many forms of a deceiver. I couldn't talk to my daddy about this lady. Who was she for real? Was she really here to help? I was told never to trust another woman. He made me see females as they were in the streets, snakes.

Phase Two taught me how to be a snake.

Phase Three

Jean was gone. I didn't trust anyone at all. Shit, I could barely trust myself. It was weird how life could change in a blink of an eye. You could go from here to there, alive to dead in a millisecond. Sometimes it was too late when I found out I made the wrong decision. By the time I realized it was the wrong thing to do, it was already done. I was a follower. I followed a man's lead. That's all I knew how to do. If Jay said Tuesday at five stay in the house because the sky was going to fall, I believed him. Tuesday at five I was in the house. I leaned on his every word. He had power over me and he was GOD in my eyes. I loved, feared, and worshiped him.

Lachelle had taken me to a motel, and we were to stay there only for one night. My daddy may have sent this freak to help me but not to help herself to his goods. She had an agenda of her own. She liked girls. I knew she was gay because she was touchy feely the moment I first met her. Then it hit me! She wanted to have sex with me. Jean has always given me insight on things I couldn't see myself. Jean explained to me how sex could be fun with a woman. I said, "How do you fuck a girl?"

My daddy taught me many ways to perform sexually. He always made me watch porn to learn special tricks which is why porn disgusts me to this day. So now I just waited on this bitch to make the first move. She did. It was easy. I blew her mind and she fell in love with me. I let her go first.

For sure I had to make a good impression, just in case she reported to my daddy. If you worked for him you knew everything was reported and done right. People did what he said or else your ass was out. She was told to make me happy and that entailed whatever and by any means. I guess it was so special that day for her. She even bought me a car the next week.

Now this bitch had a gambling problem. She couldn't keep a straight count on my daddy's money.
Plus I was robbing her blind. Jean was pissed. She

was using the money for her own selfish reasons. I'm sure he didn't have her picking up packages to gamble away.

I remember Jean being restless with this bitch and giving me precise orders to get the next stash and flee. She said she had something to show me. I was sure that what she was about to show me would be the reason why we had to steal the money and run. It was on October 7th 1985 at about five in the evening. It was warm out, still nice, not cold and definitely not hot. It was just right. Jean said "I want you to see something." She startled me just popping up out of nowhere with wild sporadic shit for us to do. My dumb ass followed suit every time.

Now it was a total no-no to go to any of the spots my daddy owned, but Jean was persistent. She had what you call a gut feeling. She made me see something I needed to see. We drove together. The nearer we got, I became more scared. I felt something wasn't right.

Jean was the bane of my existence. We

were like night and day. I loved people and only ever wanted someone to love me for me. Jean, on the other hand, was pure evil. She plotted horrible things to happen to her selected few and didn't rest until she successfully completed her goal to kill, maim, and destroy. That in itself was scary. She was never scared. That's enough to scare the shit out of anybody, especially me. She schooled me and fed me knowledge that she picked up on her own private journeys. I was in the dark a lot. Somewhat like a blackout. I would come around and didn't remember anything. Jean remembered everything. She was the brains in our relationship. I was the stunt dummy and somehow it was better than being alone.

We pulled up on Grand and Hamilton. You could get anything you wanted on Grand from drugs to sex. We ended up at one of Jay's dope spots. It was about seven in the evening. Someone was coming off my daddy's porch from copping drugs. The block no doubt was hot and crawling with all kinds of dope heads.

It was my birthday, and I knew I wasn't going to a party. It started to get dark like Jean's mood. I didn't feel special like most girls on their sweet sixteen. I was dressed in all black and my hair was tied back. When we wore black, it was lights out for someone literally. In order for Jean to complete her tasks she had to have all of me. I was keeping her from her deviance by trying to do the right thing from time to time. I had a conscious, she didn't. My only God was Jay. Jean needed to remove him so I could completely depend on her. Then she would succeed in her goal to kill me. A slow death is what she preferred. It never clicked what her plan really was.

She told me to pay close attention to the person getting out of the cab. I thought Jean was full of shit bringing me over here to see some ugly old lady get out of a damn cab. Jay had lied to me about being in jail. He was never in jail, but me being so young, I didn't know any better. Hell, I didn't even know his real name. All I was told was Jay. Plus the lesson I learned behind that was, the less I knew, the better. If I were ever questioned, I really couldn't tell anything.

When the door opened to the cab, a very dark skinned woman exited. She was so dark she looked burned. Jean nudged me, "Move your feet." She wanted me to enter the dope house with the woman. When she gave the special knock we were already at her heels. That's one thing about Jean, she was very fast. Everything she did was swift. Clearly, I had no idea that this was the bitch to replace me and he was living a secret life with. Once the door opened, Jean said, "Look quickly." I saw him on my 16th birthday inside the dining room. He had on jeans with no shirt or shoes.

He looked like he was at home. He looked comfortable standing in the center of the room with a glass thing in his hand filled with smoke. Sweat was dripping off his body like water from a shower. His eyes were bucked and he looked like he had lost weight. All this time he was here without me he had Lachelle making his runs just to keep me from being around. So he could get high with this ugly chick! He was so high that I was in the door before he could stop me. I couldn't talk because I was stunned. his man had a second life. He was a liar. I thought I was his main women but he had another all along.

She was an adult on welfare with children, and it was totally obvious she was a heavy drug user. Jay was stunned too. For a few seconds no one talked. It was an awkward moment. When he looked up from what held his undivided attention, the pipe, tears were running down my face. This chick didn't know who I was. I was sunshine, his baby. She continued on as if I was one of his customers. I looked like one too, because Jean had me wear the black get up and nothing was appealing about it. It was worn to do dirty work and that's precisely what was about to happen. Some dirty work. Her name was Mona. This bitch grabbed a wash cloth and started wiping his face. He pulled away from her and I was heated for real.

I couldn't believe what I was seeing. Jean whispered to me, "This NIGGA ain't shit! Look at her. She's dark and ugly. Her hands look like claws. Pam, she's not as pretty as you and he chose this chick to freak and get high with." I didn't get high. Hell people couldn't stand getting high with me because I always fell asleep. I couldn't handle weed and still can't to this day. Jean said, "Don't talk. Just listen to what this fool is about to tell you."

It was the first time I defied Jean. I asked my daddy, "Who is that?" My voice cracked. His bitch snapped her head up and said "Daniel Lane." She said his real name. I knew she knew him well. We're both standing in front of him waiting to hear this fantastic lie and he says, "Both of ya'll some stupid bitches." He grabbed his glass pipe and started out the door. I was in total shock at this man. He tells his door man to take care of Mona, whatever that meant. While walking past me he said, "Shine, get your ass outside." Jean was laughing while I was hurting. Wasn't shit funny. I was pissed and confused.

He was my first everything. My god, this man had taught me everything from conning a snake on the street all the way to the preacher man. Now he's showing me that I was just a pawn on a chess board. Like you'll sit here and wait until I need you. My head started spinning. I couldn't see, I felt like I was going to pass out. I got dizzier as we were leaving the spot. Jean stood up for me saying, "Listen you tired son of a bitch how dare you play with my emotions and have me with some bitch you got running for you, only for you not to be in jail. You're laying up with a junky on welfare." Before I knew it, he slapped Jean hard. Then he punched her in the face, in between her eyes, and broke her nose. He said, "Bitch I'll kill you dead for talking to me like that, you must have lost your mind. So when you find it come see me!" He pulled off in a truck I never knew he owned. I'm lost and he's gone after promptly beating Jeans ass. Jean and I were both devastated. I looked at that beat up bitch and said "You brought me over here for this shit."

I was mad but I couldn't forget that glass pipe. What was it? It seemed to have changed my daddy a lot. He wasn't as cool as before. He was racing and had slurred speech. Whatever it was, it was strong enough to take my daddy down. It was some bad shit. In the short time he was living his secret second life, he had drastically changed. Where do I go now? Do I call Lachelle? I had to help Jean. Her head was banging and there was blood everywhere. I truly couldn't remember where Mona went. I wanted to kick her ass.

I didn't learn until years later that it's never the other woman's fault. Unless you know her and she deliberately tries to take your man. But we were a surprise to each other. I hated him at that precise moment. Everything happened so fast. Jean picked herself up and dusted herself off. "This is it!!" she said and she took over.

Phase Three taught me vengeance.

Phase Four

    We jumped in the car and drove behind our old school, Highland Park High. It was secluded there. We had to think. We sat there for a minute, Jean was talking really fast. She didn't cry either. It was like a dream. I just couldn't believe what was happening. My life, as I knew it, had changed again. Jean was ready to get even. She wasn't going to rest until she did. She was pissed for real this time. I had never seen her so angry, yet I couldn't stop thinking about the glass pipe in his hand. What was it? Even with all the injuries my focus was that pipe he was holding.

    I was crying now, here I was fine and young with a chance at a decent life and he chooses this piece of bitch to play house with. Jean said we were going to the gas station. I started the car. Blood was everywhere. My shirt was pulled off. My nose was sitting slightly on the side of my face. I remember popping it back in place and pinching it to stop the bleeding. When we got to the gas station Jean grabbed the gas can, and bought another one.

She filled them both and drove back to Grand street. The black truck was gone.

My daddy owned some pit bulls, Bonnie and Clyde. He cherished them but Jean didn't care. She reached into the back seat and grabbed two empty pop bottles and started what looked to be a chemistry concoction. Her hands were shaking as she poured the gas in the bottles. I remember being hurt mentally and physically. I was jealous and furious. I wanted to hurt anyone in my path.

I had no direction. I was wild and lost. I felt completely dogged and used. I was robbed of my life and my virginity. I was told lies that gave me dreams that were never going to come true. Jay was a liar. He used me and robbed me of my innocence. He made me believe he was there to help and that he cared, but I was clearly a mule, a stunt dummy.

While Jean prepared the cocktails, I watched in terror. My eyes saw nothing but death. I only felt pain. Now someone was about to feel worse than me. Jean said, "I'll be right back. You watch for him." Of course, I followed her orders. I heard a sound I never heard before. VOOOSH!!!

The fire spread fast. She quickly did the same thing at the front door. There were only two doors and both were blocked by fire. I looked in amazement. I couldn't believe she was that evil. She didn't run back to the car. She walked slowly, like in a movie. It was slow motion. Her hair was away from her face. Her eyes were charcoal black and a bruised face. She had the sweetest yet evil look. It said, "I GOTCHA!!!"

You could hear the crackling of the wood as the house burned. Bonnie and Clyde were barking and squealing loudly. No one came running out of the house. Jean wouldn't let me leave. She wanted the house gutted with fire. She wanted his prized pits dead. Jean wanted to wipe out any life left in that house. She laughed too. I looked on with tears but you couldn't see them. They were on the inside. Jean wouldn't allow me to shed tears. She was a cold bitch. Everybody that knew her, knew it.

Even with the current horrible event in progress that glass thing was engraved in my mind. What was that and where did he get it? I was bitter, pissed, and definitely enraged all at the same time. I couldn't explain my emotions. I didn't understand what was happening. I didn't care if there were people in that house. I wanted revenge.

Jean was talking but my head was so cloudy. I could hear her, but couldn't make out the words. Too much was going on. The fire station was right down the street on Puritan and Hamilton. It didn't take long before I heard sirens. It was time to go. I was so devastated, but I really didn't feel anything. I wanted my man back. Even after all the abuse, I still wanted that nigga. Ain't that a bitch? I drove the car in reverse to the next block to prevent being seen by the authorities.

We went to my sister's house on Colfax. She lived with her twins, Darren and Danielle. I needed to hide and get myself together. My first thought was Jean. I finally took a good look at her. Her eyes were badly bruised. She looked like a line backer. My sister fixed us hot dogs with pork n beans. She really couldn't cook but that was her specialty. My sister fed me and my little brother that all the time. We still laugh about it.

We ate and slept. The next day came quickly and we needed to put another plan together. First, we had to adjust to the sun light. It really hurt our eyes from the beat down Jay gave us the day before. We wanted to know if anyone was talking about the fire. We needed to talk to Lachelle. One thing was for certain, we were on our own. I have always felt lonely. I have always been sad. I always felt like something was missing in my life. I just wasn't complete. I would trip on the people that thought I had it made. They assumed life was good for me because of what appeared on the outside. I was the dealer's girl. People thought I lived a charmed life because of what I wore and what he drove. I thought the same thing, until I went behind the scenes.

Never judge a book by the cover. Always investigate. Ask questions of yourself. I jumped into life threatening situations daily. I moved in haste, not weighing my options and definitely not looking at the consequences. Yet the lessons I learned saved my life down the line, after I banged my head a thousand times. Today, I'm still blessed to tell this story. I have learned what and what not to do.

I tried to contact Lachelle. She agreed to see me, but our meeting was about sex in her mind. Jean had Lachelle strung out. Lachelle thought we were going on a date. Jean only needed her for financial gain and of course used her for whatever she could. I told Jean she was a dirty bitch for taking me over there just to be humiliated. I started questioning Jean's friendship but I really wanted to believe in her now that my daddy was gone. She became my everything. Her plan was to have full range in my life to kill me. Her response to my verbal attack was, "I am your true friend and I will always show you the three most important sides of the game the good, the bad, and definitely the ugly. Now get ready to stroke this dingy bitch." I was shocked and hurt at this point.

I had to be game for anything and survival was a must. Lachelle acted the same as before. It was obvious she didn't know that Jay had left me. This girl had no idea about Jean. Now it was time to get dirty and stay that way. The things I learned living with my grandmother were out the window. Using proper English would have exposed that I was just a little girl who was caught up with the wrong crowd. I had to depend on Jean to carry us through. Surely gloom and doom were planned for Lachelle. She would never forget the terror that awaited her. Lachelle was in love with Jean. The thought of losing her, terrified Lachelle. It shocked me to see a woman love another woman so hard. We deliberately misused her.

Jean put together a surprise that only one of us wished never existed. Now was our chance to get my daddy's money from Lachelle and get away. Jean got Lachelle high in order to make it easy. We made love to her and robbed her completely blind. We hoped the money was still in the console of the car seeing how Lachelle had her own agenda for the money anyway. She gambled a lot but he trusted her. She trusted Jean. She got fucked. She would get that ass beating, if not killed, for the loss of his money. You couldn't survive owing him. You had to pay one way or another.

The worst thing that could ever happen to a fiend or a thief is to get caught red handed stealing from the dope man. Robbing Lachelle was easy as taking candy from a baby. She was very weak and we used her up and left her starving broke. She would be the one to go down for daddy's money. Lachelle became suspicious but Jean unplugged the motel phone and took it with her. Sure enough the money was there. It was ten thousand dollars.

I never held that much money at one time. As Jean drove, we went over the plan to get daddy to believe Lachelle fucked up his bread. Just in case we were ever questioned. He knew I would never do such a thing and I really didn't. Jean stole the money. Lachelle tried to find out what happened to Jean's face. Jean lied and blamed it on a robbery. To me it was actually a robbery. I was robbed of a normal childhood and made to believe I was loved by a man who worked elbow to elbow with the devil to break me.

I survived out there in the streets by taking other peoples hard earned money. I blamed society for the jacked up hand dealt to me. Jean made sure she had everything her way. She was taught by this demon to prey and pounce on everybody, no matter who they were, what they were doing, or what they had accomplished. She wanted to win at all cost. She didn't care who had to suffer. Everything she touched turned black. She had no feelings and I was on the run with the psycho bitch without a soul, PERIOD. She was truly the walking dead. All my life I made her my guide.

We went to McDonald's after we got the cash. I never had a caring thought about Lachelle or what she was going through. My only thoughts were of surviving. We went to Kresge's to get the things needed to live day to day.

We had absolutely no one to turn to but my

mother's sisters. We were out of options. Hell, I remember one of my aunts telling me personally how she wasn't going to take us in. Flat out she didn't want to help her dead sister's children. Of course, I didn't care for this woman. Today, I've forgiven her. Everyone has to deal with the Father, one day. She too will have her time. God said be his servant and help his children.

When I was living with the reverend, I went to church all the time. I had a hard time believing some of the things they said. The people that were supposed to follow God's request chose not to help us. God gave us the freedom to choose. I believe that my family should have given us a chance, stuck it out with us. Instead their love was given begrudgingly. The responsibility of raising us was pushed on them by my mother's death. If real love was there, I wouldn't have ended up with the dope man.

The Johnson's sent me to a home instead of trying to cope with a child who had horrible issues. Shit, back then black folks would whoop your ass.

They made you sit down somewhere and listen. But they threw their hands up with me and kept my little brother. He was the good kid. He masked his feelings while I spoke my feelings. Yet my baby brother tried to kill his self once. He drove his car into an embankment because he had some of the same horrible issues I had. He had no choice but to deal with their shit.

I, on the other hand, wasn't buying it. I knew they were only taking in Sister Lee's grandchildren, for publicity even way back then. Really, how would it look for the preacher to tell one of the eldest members of his church on her death bed, "No!!! I can't take your grandchildren." We were already lost and definitely in trouble. Today I know everything happens for a reason. I never meant to leave my baby brother though it had to be really hard for him adjusting without me. All we had was each other as kids.

Jean thought it would be best that we get our own place. With ten thousand dollars we could easily hide where no one would find us. Prior to all of these events Jay had given me information about how to receive social security income from my mother's death. I was eligible because she had a job when she passed. She was a secretary for Berry Gordy at Motown.

Imagine where we could possibly be right now had she not gotten strung out on drugs. That's the part in life when you want something really bad for another person. You would say something like "All she had to do was stay with Motown." or "She should have left this person alone." On some real shit, you have no idea what's happening in their lives or what they feel. All you see is what you want for that person and what they could have been. You don't know what really is going on with them,

Damn, it never occurred to anyone that she might have needed help. Instead they sat on the side lines and talked about a sista. Then they said to hell with her and her children. That's the way of the world.

Anyway, all I had to do was go to school to

receive my mother's hard earned money. The computer system was not remotely advanced like it is today. They still had me active as a student. I wish I had finished school. I still don't have my GED. We had to change the address so it would come straight to me. We both knew once the stolen money was gone we would need a steady income.

While I rested, Jean went to the social security office to make sure we would have an income. That's how we survived. One would rest while the other worked. We would take turns in my life. I always knew who I was or should I say what I was. We needed an address. Jean sat in the car and put together a plan. She was the planner. I was a wimp. I always took the rap when we were caught. So most times I just hoped things went well.

I woke up that morning with the sun beaming on my face. Somehow I knew there was a GOD because no matter what, I woke up every day. We slept in the car. It seemed like every time I turned around, I was living in the streets, in a car, crashing here and there. We had to spend this money wisely. Jean and I lived in the car for a few days. We tried to sleep in the safest areas in the city. I went back to Hampton Dr. once because it was a familiar place. That's where my little brother continued to stay with the Bishop family. I missed David. I wanted to see him. I wondered how he was doing. We had not seen each other in years. I looked at the house. It didn't seem that big now. I felt like asking for help and just couldn't without feeling stupid. Uncle David had helped us.

    I needed help to get my new place when I was pregnant with my first born child. We needed a home to bring Jamarie from the hospital. My son's father and I went to Hope Baptist Church on Seven Mile Rd. to ask for the remaining down payment on the house. Uncle David didn't hesitate. He gave us the money. I loved him. A lot people in Detroit loved him then and still do.

    I was afraid Jean would hurt his wife. Had she said anything stupid to me concerning how we got the money, it would have been on. We never went back to that mansion on Hampton Drive. I missed my brother a lot.

It was terrible when we separated. I love my little brother. He will always be that to me even though he hates me. God has to deal with him as well. I have had nothing but losses my entire life. My mother, my brothers and sister, and even not knowing who my real father is, was a loss.

Hell, I even lost my own life. I didn't die physically but a part of me died. Being alone had become easy. I learned at a young age to be a loner. I had old faithful Jean. She was fun until I found out she was trying to kill me. That's when the battle began.

Phase Four taught me to be true to myself.

Phase Five

Jean made sure we were safe. She had to keep me in one piece in order to complete her mission. Now as the sun beamed, so did Jean. She said, "Wake up, Sunshine. Today is the day you get your own home. I got the money but I need your class." I learned how to speak articulately as a young girl from my grandmother. She was very good with words and could mingle with the best. Sunshine was the nickname my daddy gave me. My real name was Pamela Marshall.

We looked for rental properties in the newspaper. We found a four family flat on Elmhurst and Linwood. We could have taken everything from Lachelle including her car. My daddy's money was gone and his prized pits were dead. His trap houses were shut down and as far as I was concerned. I was still trying to find my mind. I really wasn't ready to see him. Plus, we were not in the mood for another fight just yet. Once he came down off his high long enough to realize we had hit him hard, someone was going to die. We would fight to save our life if we had to. This place was a nice distance from Highland Park. No one would think to find us there. It was just me and Jean, the dark angel, my only friend. She made me see I didn't need anyone but her.

It was time to find some other resources. I needed someone to guide me. If someone had told me what Jean had in store for me, I would have told them that they were a lie. I loved her so much and I believed in her and as much as I missed my man. She wouldn't let me fold. She constantly reminded me of how he would beat my ass. Wasn't I tired of that? I would stare into space and agree.

Jean and I got closer. We were one. We laughed, cried, ate, slept, and did everything together, including sex. At the time, I couldn't live without her. I knew I had family on my father's side, well the man who I thought was my father's side. We had to find them. It was a Saturday morning, and we were both wracking our brains trying to locate them. I already knew it was a no go on my mother's side. They didn't have any love for me.

They chose to help my sister, Lonnie. She was the debutante queen. She went to New York on her senior trip. She then went on to college. My sister always had nice clothes, pretty little do dads, and such. Hell!! She even owned ice skates! Very few black people had ice skates, but she did. My sister had it all.

I love my sister. My mother's sisters allowed me and my siblings to be separated. We were considered excess baggage. Their lives were more important. As an adult today, I still believe they were wrong. Especially when they look at me like tisk, tisk, tisk, ain't that a bitch? They don't even know where my mother is buried. No one ever put flowers on her grave. She doesn't even have a headstone. But they judge me and my life. I guess out of sight, out of mind.

That is what happens when you think you're better than someone else, especially people who have an addiction to drugs. They still judge her to this day. I won't allow my children to talk about anyone less fortunate, because I have been there. My siblings and I suffered because of my mother's lifestyle. My children suffered because of my lifestyle. The only difference was my brothers helped me. I thank my brothers for stepping up for me. God knows just how much I really appreciate them. It was a repeat. Talk about generational curse. My mother had six sisters, and not one helped us.

Jay taught me that family will be the first ones to get you. Today I have acceptance. Yet it still hurts. I wonder how they feel today. Especially knowing God is going to judge them, in the exact same manner.

Crazy things happen in life. Why did this happen to me? "Damn, you know why, for some shit your ass did in the past", Jean snapped me out of my thoughts. When I told her my thoughts, her response was, "Fuck them. They will reap. I'll make sure of it." Whenever Jean spoke anything, it happened. She was very vindictive. I looked at her in amazement. Nothing bothered her. She had no feeling, what so ever. It was as if she was the devil himself. She made black magic appealing. I thought she had a gift of power. I was scared of her, especially when she was pissed, but I loved Jean. I just didn't know she didn't love me. Now after three days in this car, it was finally time to go see the new house.

We went to meet someone about it. There was a big red for rent sign in the window. The area was decent. There was a church across the street and a gas station on the corner. We parked and got out the car. It looked okay, kind of on the raggedy side, but we needed a place right now, so it would have to do. We knocked on the door. A light skinned brother answered the door with tools in his hand. We introduced ourselves and he told us his name was Mr. Taylor.

We got straight to business. I have always been like that. He wanted seven hundred dollars for the first month's rent and security deposit. Jean and I looked at each other and thought it was fair and cashed the man out. At our age it wasn't heard of to have your own place. We couldn't let him know how old we were, so without a second thought we gave Mr. Taylor more money to eliminate a paper trail of any kind. Jay would surely find us once he found out about his money and dogs. Jay had a way of finding things out.

Mr. Taylor was a nice man. He had sandy brown hair and freckles. He was kind of stocky but you could tell he was cute in his day. He looked at us peculiar because all the transactions were done before we even saw the inside. He tried to show it to us twice before taking our money. But of course money talks and bullshit walks. That was another lesson I learned from Jay. Anyone could be bought and/or sold, if the price was right. He was not lying.

This man surely knew he was dealing with a minor. The money kept him from even prying for more information. I looked old enough to do anything I wanted. I could even buy alcohol whenever I felt like drinking. Now every month we were to pay him $350 dollars. Our agreement was sealed when we paid the man for a year in advance to assure us a roof. No telling where we would end up if we couldn't pay our rent. So that was the deal. We were given a set of keys and told about the remaining work that needed to be done on the house. He would be back and forth periodically. I was excited and felt like a grown up for real.

Life seemed to be easier without Jay, but I missed him. It was stressful most times and downright scary all the time. The love I received from him was bad love. I didn't know it then but today I know it wasn't love at all. As we walked around the flat we made a list of everything needed. We bought it all, from the front door to the back. It had not dawned on me that I would have to pay bills. I had never done that before. This was my first time being responsible for anything in my life. But we would worry about that later. Jean said she wanted to look around the neighborhood. We left the flat and got familiar with the stores and the neighborhood.

It's amazing when you have money. You

don't seem to have worries. You can shake the ground, buy what you want, eat what you want, go where you want and live good too. I thought I was that girl. I was doing it all by myself with the help of my right hand, Jean.

I didn't know where I would have been without her. As I sat in the store parking lot, I thought about how I missed Jay and wished he could see me now. Jean interrupted, "Yeah he would be kicking your ass and make you go back with him." I learned the hard way about a controlling man. If you ever left him and were doing good, he would definitely try to break your stride showing nothing but jealousy. She said, "He only wants to control you." All we had left to do was decorate our new place. That would keep us busy making the house a home. Jean and I were inseparable; we did everything together at that time.

We had neighbors in our four family flat and it was painfully obvious all of them were on some kind of drug. The guy across the hall never spoke and neither did we. After we were settled in our new apartment I went to see my sister. Jean thought it best to find my family through her. My sister gave me my aunt's number on my father's side of the family. This is the family Jean wanted me to be involved with, my basehead cousins. They were all addicted to drugs. She knew I would like them. They seemed fun and acted like they cared.

I called my dad's oldest sister, Nina Yarbrough. To my aid she came and she still will to this day. She's just a phone call away. She is the picture perfect citizen. Never been in jail, or used drugs. She was never mean to me. She always smiled and never judged me. She wanted a better life for me. She knew my mom and the trouble we would endure long before I met her. I love that lady with all my heart. She was the only one who came to see about me. I will never forget those beautiful bath towels, pots and pans she gave me as house warming gifts.

I found out about my oldest brother Curtis through my aunt. He was living in an abandoned building on Beachwood near the 96 freeway service drive. I told Jean I'm going to get my brother. Something was tugging me his way. This building wasn't fit for your average street hoe. It was horrible! It had broken windows, no doors, no food or appliances, just a rat infested, roach populated hell hole. Curtis would sleep using two chairs pushed together. To make a long story short, Curtis came home with me. I gave my brother the back bedroom. We barely knew each other and he definitely didn't know Jean. We met the neighbors upstairs around the same time. Yet, Curtis stayed to himself. If you didn't know for certain he was there, you wouldn't have known. Curtis was and still is a quiet man, never bringing attention to himself. I can honestly say that my brother loves me very much; he has always wanted the best for me. I love him so much!

The couple that lived above us was based out, completely gone off drugs. The same stuff my daddy used in that glass pipe. It seemed like everyone was using it. They had a lot of kids, maybe five of them. They had been married a long time. Their children were unkempt, very raggedy, and with the saddest eyes I had ever seen. It was truly fucked up. They begged for everything. I used to help them. Jean laughed at horrible occurrences. She thought she was better than most people. She laughed at shit that the average person wouldn't remotely find funny. She would be pissed when I looked out for those kids.

Anyway all of the traps were set and everyone was in place, except my dumb ass. I never saw any of it coming. It was Indian summer. I was about to turn seventeen. I had my car parked in front running. my Mrs. Thomas, the one who was married and had all the children, called me up to her flat. "Here Pam, pull this", she said. Against my better judgment I pulled the smoke from the famous glass pipe that had held my interest since I saw my daddy with one.

She told me to hold the smoke. I did but I was in a hurry. I left still holding the smoke in my mouth. Once in the car, I blew it out. I turned the corner, came back around, and ran up the stairs asking how much and where can I find it. It seemed like every nerve in my body came alive. It tasted so damn good. It immediately erased any pain I may have had mentally and physically. It heightened my awareness completely.

Every since I saw my daddy with that pipe, I wanted one too. Mrs. Thomas was more than eager to take me to get the stuff. This was my start to sudden death, hell, damnation, and a life of unstoppable danger.

Phase Five was hard. I became an addict.

Phase Six

I changed drastically. The wimp in me was gone, instantaneously. I felt incredibly vicious. I was getting that pipe!!! There was a gas station that sold them a few blocks away on Dexter and Waverly. Jean sat still with a very eerie silence. She would normally have input on everything I did. She controlled everything and now this wretched bitch has absolutely nothing to say.

I could feel she was pleased with the current events. She was satisfied that anything in me that was still pure was about to be tainted and gone forever after this day. When the lady from upstairs came back to the car she handed me the most beautiful glass I ever seen in my life. I was ecstatic, now where do I get the shit I said. She gave anxious directions, of course she was going to score for hooking me up, and hell I was anxious too. I wanted some more of that good shit right now. This drug had the power of a God, immediately multiple changes occurred in my life physically and mentally.

We went to the store on the opposite side of the street of the gas station to score. She copped the stuff from this really cute guy who looked to be my age. When she got back in the car and handed me three big white rocks, I looked at her like she was crazy. "What's this?" I said, she said "it's the dope". I said "like this", it looked like those decorative rocks you would see in some ones well manicured yard it had a crystal shine to it.

As I held all of this stuff in my hands it looked like a chemistry set, it seemed like too much to do to get high. Very different from weed, twist and smoke, but with this, you had to put the pipe together and the rock was so hard to break it would hurt your fingers. You had to use a blade of some kind. It wasn't that expensive, but the taste of it had my wheels rolling. When we got back to the flat we sat down all three of us to prepare for that massive blast I got the first time, and it never came again.

After the pain staking procedure was done, the lady from upstairs finally put me a piece of the rock onto the screen that held it. Then she dipped a piece of rod with cotton at the end into a top that had 151 proof Bacardi in it. This shit was starting to piss me off, or maybe I was too anxious. But here is the kicker, she kept lighting it and just letting me pull out the smoke after her. She was just using me. She was getting high but I wasn't, not like she was.

Jean told me after a couple hours of silence, "Pay attention to this bitch. She's using you. Watch her flow. She thinks you're slow. Let me help you Pam", she said.

So I stepped down and let Jean in. Let the games begin. This lady doesn't know me. Jean went into our funds. We went back to that store and found the dope boy. We got the dope, went home, and locked the door. Curtis wasn't home. We got high as a Dittrich fur. For some strange reason, I felt dirty like I was doing something wrong. I felt like I was losing something deep within me as I was exhaling smoke. I felt ashamed of myself. I was losing my soul and my spirit at the same time.

As I inhaled I pulled in filth and devilment.

I couldn't move. It started sucking up my mind immediately. My only thought now was how to stay supplied with this new found ecstasy I was experiencing. I felt devious and dangerous. There weren't any pleasant thoughts, just plans and schemes. There weren't soft voices in my head. They were all rude and loud. Jean loved getting high. She felt right at home in the defiance. She was so hyped on destructive forces. She had major plans for us.

The first thing I needed to do was to get back in good with my daddy. He had more than enough of this stuff to keep us high or just flat out stealing it was an option. Jean didn't care. She was ready to start the mission. I went for the ride. It was the taste that got me. Jean wanted me driven so she could get in and stay in until the mission was complete. That was my death. I decided to ride the demonic roller coaster. The drug made me forget things that were unwanted and painful. I was in a daze. I wanted to stay that way.

How we were going to do it was left up to

Jean. After a week of this non-stop high, we were down to our last two hundred dollars and that too was about to belong to the dope boy. I never saw how we kept him paid while we were sucking ourselves dry. None of that matters at the precise moment you're using. All you seem to see is the smoke. But when it clears, you feel like the dumbest person that ever walked the face of the earth. I had gotten to the point where I wouldn't even share this shit with anyone.

So now that we were on our last, Jean started probing in an area she knows I detested. She asked, "Pam, don't you miss your mom?" I immediately started crying. I knew she was trying to blow my high. I was already pissed, heartbroken, and extremely depressed, all at the same time. Once she got started talking, Jean wouldn't shut up.

I wondered about my mom a lot. What did she wear? Was she fun or did she even have any fun? Did she have a lot of friends? I just wanted to know what she was like. How could you miss what I never had? The more I thought, the more I smoked. My feelings were numb. I wanted to ask her a bunch of questions. Why did she leave us and what happened the day of her murder? I'm sure no one knows that information but her and her killer. She didn't live long. She was twenty nine years old when she was killed. I used to think twenty nine was old, until I turned twenty nine. Jean asked me what was wrong. I told her nothing. She knew damn well what was wrong. I just kept crying and smoking.

My life just kept getting lonelier and lonelier. The madness had only just begun. On my eighteenth birthday, October, 7th, I still wasn't ready to see my daddy. For sure, he knew about his house and dogs. With all his scandalous teachings, it couldn't have been anyone but me. He had seen Jean in action although he never met her personally. I would never do anything to harm him, even though he would send me on various missions that could have very well killed me. That's why I always sent Jean.

Every birthday as far back as I could

remember was FUCKED UP. Now on this birthday I clearly was at my best. As usual I was dressed to kill. No one has ever seen me out of order, even to this day. I took major pride in my appearance. I had a kick for parties. I had never had a party. I wanted to look good and have a party of my own. I didn't have any friends. I was going to get high and kick it around with a few people I came across in my addiction. Before I could get cool, the mail lady was coming up the street. I never expected this to happen. The big check finally came. It was a nice start to my birthday. It was my mother's money, $2300. Man, I was so geeked up! I ran and told my brother.

    I never had an I.D. I had no real use for one. The money was needed and this check had to be cashed. My brother took me to a check cashing place on Oakman near Grand River. When we walked in, they made me an I.D. and cashed my check. I surprised my brother and gave him one thousand dollars. We went to Northland mall. Curtis went shopping. Jean and I shopped, and shopped lifted. When we returned home, we got completely intoxicated. I didn't see my brother for a few days and we were living in the same house.

I didn't know how to budget and spent money like there wasn't a tomorrow. I'm still like that to this day. When I thought I should buy food, Jean came with her brand of logic, get high and stay high. I never could eat while using cocaine. The weight fell of me like sweat off of a boxing champ.

Jean never allowed moments of clarity to sink in and she made sure I recognized the special little things this stuff did to me. It made me horny and it made me sleep with many for plenty of money. Robbery was my real hustle. I would rather take your shit then lie down and fuck.

It was a euphoria that I couldn't explain. At the same time, it was something demonic that had seeped in my veins. It ran through my blood. It pumped into my brain. I was ready to do more and ready to commit murder for it. I couldn't believe how frantic I became without it. I became a monster inside. A piece of white rock that had no brain, could not walk, or talk, made decisions for me. Seriously, it ruled my life. As time continued to go on, it didn't dawn on me, that my childhood was gone. There weren't any sleepovers, doll houses, girl talks, high school pep rallies, or prom. It was all about the streets, hell games, violence, and drugs. Nothing was fun. Everything was dangerous.

Jean was just as messed up as me. As time came and went, so did my obsession. It was time to see the monster that was inside me. Because I was hopelessly in love with Jay, Jean thought it best she represent us. I was so gone for him, like a groupie at a Run DMC concert. She had more strength and looked at him as nothing more than a lick. This would be easy for her, but for me, it would be challenging. We drove in silence. His mom lived on Monterey in Highland Park. We knew he would be around at some point. Jean was very pretty and had a serious sex appeal that was alluring to most men.

But this man looked at her as business and I never knew it. Once I found out, it wouldn't have mattered to me but it did to her. She had long dark hair with beautiful ocean waves. Her eyes were like black diamonds and they glistened only in the center. Her teeth were perfect, white like ivory. Her skin was a rich caramel. Shit, she was a living doll! Yet, deep inside, she was a voodoo doll sent straight from the devil in hell himself, to take my soul. It seemed she had my best interest at heart but deep down she didn't. She could turn the simplest thing into a catastrophe.

Going to the grocery store with her could turn into an armed robbery. All we had to do was shop for what we needed but a dark gloom would suddenly appear. We would be jacked up and locked up. Back then jail was easier. It was called larceny from a building. You'd probably get probation. But while this twisted bitch never got charged, I always did. We rarely got caught but when we did, I had to do the time.

It became obvious she didn't care about me. We were waiting like sitting ducks for this man to show up and kick ass on site. Suddenly, a beautiful red Pontiac with a white rag top appeared. I became a little nervous. It was almost like meeting a super star or something. I just didn't know how to act. He would sometimes say that I would never be anything or I couldn't do anything without him. He would see I could make it without him. So we looked our best. I was wearing all the jewelry he bought me only for the unthinkable to happen.

When he got out the car I yelled, "DADDAAAAY!!!!!!!!!" He turned around with fire jetting from the top of his head and steam coming out his ears. This man was coming to kill. We had been set up by Lachelle. She was bitter at Jean for not being true in the relationship. This man still wanted my head. He was the guillotine. Before I knew it, he was at the car beating me to a pulp. He was still furious even though it had been months since the fire. It was time to leave him alone but I really didn't know how to do it. What was even worse, I didn't even want to do it. He was all I knew. He was my everything. I had bad nightmares from the abuse. My dreams were so real. Just the thought of him being completely done with me was insane.

My face blew up instantly like helium in a balloon. He was calling me names I had never heard. That hurt more than the assault. I felt like I had done nothing wrong. I became furious with myself for listening to Jean. I ended up practically in traction because of her.

People started coming out of their homes. Small children were crying for me. I was beaten so badly, I needed medical attention. Every time I healed from an episode, there was another. The scars on the inside took longer to heal than the ones on my face. I was naked from the waist up, publicly humiliated, physically beaten, mentally exhausted, and completely deserving of something better. Out of all the people who witnessed the assault, only one man helped. How could anyone watch a 250 pound man beat on a 120 pound teenager? I remember him saying he's not done with me yet, that I would pay, as if I had not suffered enough. He had taken my jewelry again, he always gave it back after awhile, but this time it was over.

I learned the hard way about how some men use material things to lure you in to their little trap. They fill your head with illusions and lies only to benefit sexually. It was many years after him I found out not all men were like him. I didn't know how to keep a man who wasn't like him. I ran away the men that were decent and kept the ones who dogged the shit out of me.

There were so many men that were full of it. I got to the point where I didn't want to even risk happiness because of so many failed attempts trying to find it. This time he managed to break my nose bad enough that it had to be repositioned. He could have killed me. Getting hit in the face is actually traumatizing, especially when the person has hands that are huge and heavy.

This was a time I could have really used Jean and this trick never showed up. It was the first time I wished I could kill her. She would purposely take me to a death trap and leave me. I learned how to block out pain long before drugs came into play. For me, being hard and feeling nothing was easy. There was nothing else to do at this time so I prayed that he would stop hitting me and he did. WOW!!!!!! Where did that instant help come from? I drove away alone, totally alone. A cold chill lingered in the car even though I was a few blocks away from the assault.

    I knew I would never see him again. For some reason I couldn't cry. It's funny how people can come into your life for a time, for whatever reason, either you learn something or you don't. I had learned so much through the years we were together. I was twenty years old when I finally got over him. I stayed with him from fourteen until I was twenty. In that time my education was given to me from the devil himself. I was a girl, then instantly a woman!

    Yet, I was so far from being a lady. I never really saw a real lady, except on TV. I thought they were all in church. I thought ladies were all my Grandmother's age. I had to be old before I became one. I was once told a real lady doesn't do drugs. As the years continued to come and go, I used drugs every day. It was kind of like taking a bath, I got high every day. I learned that what he and I shared wasn't love. Hell, I didn't know real love to be able to tell the difference. This love hurt but the word love is so beautiful. It didn't seem like it should have felt like that. It was painful, stressful, and depressing.

      I used to be scared that I was going to do or say the wrong things. No man loves you when you're to be sold for his financial gain. No man loves you when he breaks your face and shatters your spirit. No man loves you when you're verbally thrashed if he feels it necessary and you've done nothing but wake up. No man loves you when the sight of you gets under his skin. Jay definitely was not a man!! Just because he had a penis didn't make him a man, it made him a male. He was shot many years later doing what he did best, being the dope man.

      He robbed me of a chance at a decent life.

At his age, he knew better then to guide me in that direction. Instead of helping me, he helped himself. Later he was robbed of one of Gods most precious gifts, the use of his legs. Now he can't walk. Talk about GOD having vengeance, the Lord said "Let vengeance be mine".

We've had small conversations since I was a kid. He even helped me while I was in prison. Dig this, he looked me up on Otis, that's the offender tracking system, he stopped writing me. He said I was ugly. Anyone in their right mind would think any mug shot is ugly. Yet to base a friendship on ones looks in an uncomfortable situation is sad.

I was further educated about humans, how shallow minded a person could be. There was never anything wrong with me. There was something very wrong with him. The beatings, the lies, and everything else, was stored in my mental files. The next man wouldn't have that chance, ever.

Every man suffered horribly after him. They were misused and were treated with no respect. I definitely had no regard for their feelings. As a matter of fact, I dared a man to hit me. I tried to kill anyone who did. I was to the point where they left me alone. I stayed single. I was more of a man then most of them. Believe it or not, most men were intimidated by me. Some still are to this day. I tell you, between Jay and Jean, I was mentally shattered, beyond repair, and needed severe psychological counseling.

    I had become just like him. He was my first introduction to real life, straight from the gutter and everything that fit in that category. It had been a rough five years. I can't really remember anything good other than this puppy I had found on the North End of Detroit on one of my many capers. Someone left it in a box on the sidewalk. I picked it up and took it home.

    I named her Queen. It was a lonely time for me after living in the car and leaving Jay. Queen brought joy to me. She loved me no matter what. Animals just love you, for loving them. They don't judge. I needed love and Queen loved me for taking her out of that box.

Phase Six taught me about real love.

Phase Seven

Christmas had come and gone. I had been without sex for a few months. I had been in jail so much it had become really easy to go without it. I hadn't slept with a man or a woman. I had become a career criminal. I had hit all kinds of jobs with Jean. I was always looking for a victim. I remember this guy walking up our street dressed like a mechanic. He was a potential victim for sex or robbery. He had the look of Little Richard with his perm and finger waves. He had a different kind of swag and he made me laugh. In my life, rarely was anything funny. Everything was serious.

Soon after I began dating this guy, I learned he was a liar. By now, you know I can't stand for a man to lie to me. He said he was single. But, he wasn't. He definitely had a girlfriend. I found out because she was at the card party he invited me to at his sister's house. Marie was very pretty and sweet to me. No matter what she heard about me, she was still my friend.

There's always some shit that stinks. This time it was his. I think men who want a variety of women should just say so. Why lie about it? He could have said, "Look, I got a girl. I just want to fuck you sometime." or "We're broke up right now. Let's just kick it awhile." That's how I know I'm different. You could be 3 feet tall with one eye, protruding gums, look like you lived in a dumpster behind a restaurant, and be smelled before you hit the corner, just keep it straight up and don't get on Jean's bad side. We'll be fine. I love people, but like Michael Jackson says, they want to be starting something.

There were people everywhere in this little bitty house. One girl stuck out like a sore thumb. She was beautiful. She had skin that was like a perfectly blended peach. She also had the prettiest smile. She was just downright fine. This girl had class. Everything about her was like the ocean. It could be easy or it could get rough. It could get nasty and yet it could give you peace.

What was really amazing though, was this girl was

about to jump on me about this no nothing ass fool. I can't really remember how it went down. She knew he had brought me to the party. I know we didn't fight. We instantly became friends. She was all that to me and to this day she's my best friend. She wore nothing but the best. She had a flair of her own. She had something I always wanted, a family. When the card game was over, so was our relationship with that fool. Neither one of us ended up with him.

Meeting Iris Lynn Hill was the one good thing to come out of that situation. Everyone called her Lynn. My life at this time seemed to be moving fast. Lynn's parents lived on the west side of Detroit on Murray Hill. It was a really nice neighborhood. They had a lovely home. I had never seen a family so close. Every family has problems, but you couldn't tell it with the Hill family.

Lynn's dad was the picture perfect dad. He died at the age of 92, rest his soul. You never heard him shouting or cussing at his children. He was a hard working, GOD fearing, unselfish man and took care of his family. He was a father figure to many. The home was cozy and very clean. Mrs. Hill ran the house and she made sure it ran efficiently.

I will never forget the first meal I ate there. We had roast beef, macaroni and cheese, green beans, homemade dinner rolls, and peach cobbler. Talk about cooking! She could have been rich from just making a meal. My girl Lynn treated me like a sister. She saw that I was a tom boy and that I could take or leave the glamorous stuff. After dinner we went to her room. She lived in Mother Hill's basement. This was no ordinary basement. In fact, you couldn't tell it was a basement. One side was completely decorated like a boutique. The kind where you have a seat and the assistant brings out the best the store has to offer. On the other side it looked more like an apartment. That's where my transformation started. Lynn got busy on me from the top of my head to the bottom of my feet.

She showed me sisterly love and she made it clear I couldn't use this shit around her either.

She knew I got high and she still befriended me. Lynn didn't care. I guess she saw something in me and it didn't matter to her what my past was or what I did in my day to day life.

Jean she didn't like my friend much. She hated healthy relationships. She saw how Lynn and I were becoming close. Lynn was about to be an asset in my life. She was showing me another side of life. I saw how life could and should be. I remember our first real heart to heart. After dinner Lynn told me a few secrets about her family. She told me what she wouldn't tolerate from anyone who was her friend. She said, "Pam you're going to be a lady around me and you can't use that stuff." She wasn't a drug user.

Lynn showed me how not to bite my nails and gave me manicures. She did my hair. She showed me her closet. This lady had the whole department store right there: clothes, shoes, accessories, every color hand bag, stockings, jewelry, and such. To the right was a beauty salon. She had the chair, tables, and mirrors. All kinds of hair care products. She even had an appointment book. People came from all around for this girl to do their hair. I felt special to be her friend. She always made me feel good about myself. She never treated me like she was better than me or like I was a poor case.

Lynn did all she did for me out of the kindness of her heart. She pampered me and touched me like she had hands of a child soft and sweet. She was my friend. Jean knew she had no win at Lynn's place. she would get her ass beat for real. My friend was a fighter like me. That girl had a famous reach out and touch your ass right hook that you would never see coming. You would just find yourself getting off the floor. It was the first time I saw Jean had no control.

She was never too far away. She would try to convince me that Lynn was treating me nice only to let me down later. Jean said "People have no real love for others. They just use you for what you can do for them". Yet that didn't sit right with me. I could sense Lynn being genuine every step of the way. Lynn wasn't a fake. She was just as real as me. I never told anyone about Jean, especially Lynn. I wanted her friendship. She made me feel good about myself and the changes I was making. She made me want to be better. I couldn't introduce Jean to her. Jean scared people away and I wasn't going to lose the only person who I felt loved me for real.

Lynn took the time to show me things no one ever did about my personal grooming. I watched her carefully. Lynn showed me how to keep myself up. She was smooth. Jean wanted to keep me from good people and she would find ways to do it. When Lynn was out of town with her man, me and Jean would get high. This particular weekend Lynn and her man, Dana, went on a plane to Chicago. They went to do some shopping. They were always doing something. Dana was a big time dealer out of southwest Detroit. He would do things for her and for me that were unreal. We went to fine dining, movies, concerts, and other things. He treated her like a lady. He treated her how a man should treat a woman.

When Lynn and I weren't together I always managed to get in some kind of mischief. Thanks to Jean's chronic ass. This night Jean suggested we go to The Locker Room, a bar on Livernois. Jean wanted us to hang alone for a while, plus it was a chance for me to dress in some of the things my girl Lynn got me.

I chose a black dress that had splits all around the bottom of the dress. It tied around the neck and it was low cut in the front with the back out. I was stunning and impressed with myself. All of the accessories matched and my hair was pinned up with spiral curls around the front and sides. I looked elegant. In fact I should have been going to the Ritz. Jean thought it best we have a few drinks before going. She asked if I felt like getting buzzed. I said, "Why not?" We had some money, enough to get us a nice amount of drugs to last for the night. When we got high, we got high big. We scored our drugs and hit the set.

Inside the bar it was wall to wall people, big people, little people, cute people and ugly people. It was the first time I went to a club. I saw the flip side of church. Everyone was dancing, laughing loud, and just doing their thing. Everyone seemed dressed extremely casual. This was a neighborhood bar and I felt over dressed. But the alcohol kicked in and everything seemed to be fun, especially taking a hit of cocaine in the bathroom.

Jean couldn't help herself. She did what she wanted, when she wanted, and fuck who was watching. A very cute guy he kept staring at me. Jean said, "Fuck him. Let's go out to the parking lot." I knew how to shut her up. I just wouldn't respond. It was the only way to have some kind of control of my own mind. I learned how to keep her silent. I just didn't know how to keep her down. She was very strong. We were always looking for a victim. I would lure them and Jean would get them.

We tag teamed in just about every caper. This one was on me. I was attracted to this stranger. He was 6 feet 4 inches tall and he weighed about 240 pounds. It was all muscle. He had a dangerous six pack and had the cutest bowlegged walk. His jeans were perfectly creased and he had on a muscle shirt. He smelled so good. His name was Jeffery Wilson. I liked him and it surprised me, seeing how I had just been in a horrible relationship with Jay. I wanted this man. It didn't matter if he had money or not. He was nice to me. He seemed different. We danced and got along well.

He told me he wanted to keep in touch, and of course we did. We spent the rest of the evening together. After a week into the new friendship, Jean and I went on a shopping spree. We would do that from time to time. We couldn't get just one item of anything, we needed twenty items or better. We had to pay bills and being an addict didn't help. We constantly needed money. I called it shopping, when it's clearly shop lifting. This time it wasn't successful.

I went to jail. I didn't mind going. It allowed my body time to heal from the daily abuse of the drugs. As usual, Jean abandoned me.

It was just me dealing with the Oakland County Jail. They were light on me. They gave me six months in a work release program. To my surprise, Jeff came every visiting day with my brother Curtis. We were in love. But I still thought of Jay every day.

Phase Seven taught me about friendship.

Phase Eight

Shortly after my release, I got pregnant with my first born child, Jamarie. We picked his name out of an African book. It means brave. Only God knew that later in his life he would really have to be. Jean was pissed I had stopped smoking cocaine. I had to quit. I was afraid for my child's life. But this demon didn't care. Jean doesn't sleep, she only rests. On October 30, 1989 my joy was born.

I never had friends. There wasn't a baby shower, but between Lynn and Jeff, I didn't need one. Everything my baby needed and more was provided by them. I was grateful because physically I couldn't do anything. I was extremely sick carrying him. My pregnancy had taken a toll on my body.

My little boy was so gorgeous. He was a living doll. I never wanted to be away from him. I breast fed him. The nurses in the hospital said it would be better for the baby and it was. My son never got sick. He didn't have cradle cap and maybe threw up twice in his life. He weighed 7 pounds 10 ounces and he looked just like his father. He was a little person. He had everything we had, just smaller. He was my special child. I remember being sad a lot. I didn't want this chaotic bitch to ruin my new life with my son.

The week he was born Jean came home ready to party. Our parties were never fun. They started out cool, but ended dangerous and devastatingly scary. I was changing my little man when she startled me. She spoke softly, "He's so pretty." It was eerie the way she spoke at that moment. She wasn't a soft spoken person. Everything she did was harsh, especially her words. I looked down at my baby, at that moment Jean and I talked, my son, he seemed to have glared through me like he knew I was full of shit. It wasn't me, it was Jean, I could tell my son could see her.

I felt he could feel danger among us. I really wanted Jean to go away. She tainted everything and she wasn't going to stop because I had a child. I had tears streaming down my face,

"Jean go away." She said with a hint of sass and sarcasms "NEVER!!!!!!!" I said, "Jean not right now, this boy needs me." She cleared her throat, and with a stern conviction said, "So do I." I cried silently and rocked my baby to sleep. I knew she meant what she said; she always did. I feared her so much. I was scared for myself and especially my son. I stayed clean for a while. But that didn't last long. She made sure of it. August of 1990 was when I started getting cool again.

I shared a three family flat with my Dad, Mr. Lloyd Marshall on the right side of me and Mr. Ali stayed downstairs. Mr. Ali was definitely one of God's angels. He was very helpful with my son. He had taken me to my doctor's appointments and anywhere else I had to be. He had a crush on me. He was a sweet old man and a Muslim very committed to his religion. He treated me like a queen. Jeff and I were on shaky ground. He was at the point where he could not take the violent arguing.

I had wild out burst from time to time. I

didn't have a clue they were symptoms of withdrawal. I had never tried to stop getting high before, so I didn't know what I was going through. He had picked up heavy drinking and it clearly didn't work out. He left us and went to Ohio where his mom lived. She had fallen sick and he went to help her. Now that the main bread winner was gone and my social security was over, I had nothing.

I was 21 years old and not in school. I had to turn to welfare. Jean was working around the clock removing the positive people out of my life. They disappeared left and right. She flat out ran them away. Even Curtis found him a nice girl to take up with, her name was Fannie. Life seemed normal but it really wasn't. It still trips me out when I ask myself to define normal.

I can't say that I ever experienced normal living; what is normal living anyway? Jean made it very hard for me. All she wanted to do was get high and die trying. I had reached the point where I dreaded my birthdays. All kinds of weird shit would happen to me during October. I had just turned 22 years old and as usual I didn't do anything but get high. Jamarie's 1st birthday was approaching. He would be one year old on October 30th

I went to the gas station on Dexter and Waverly, where I got my first bowl from to cop some loose cigarettes. They were 10 cents each. It was close to Halloween. It was kind of scary looking around that time of year, especially where I lived. I decided to dress like a boy to prevent from being approached by the night crawlers of the neighborhood. It didn't work. There was a man on the corner of my street who looked like a black Groucho Marx, with thick bushy eye brows, black thick rimmed glasses, and his mustache was thick and black as well. He had on a dark blue suit with a beige trench coat.

He was sporting a hat that a golfer would wear, with wild hair sticking out only on the sides. Apparently he had followed me. It was my turn. I was always hunting for prey but I was someone's prey this night. He was hiding behind a huge dump truck that blocked the end of the alley.

All I saw was a huge hole staring me in my face. This gun had to be a forty five caliber. It had been years since I had a piece pointed at me, Santa's wife. I stood completely still. I had no weapon, no gangster buddy, as usual this bitch was nowhere in sight. It was just me, the predator, and his big black gun. He said, "Get in." and shoved me slightly. He made me get in on the driver's side. That alone told me this man was not playing with me.

My first words were "Please don't kill me." I don't remember being scared. I was pissed and worried about my son. All I could see was my son at home alone with Mr. Ali. It was October 17, 1990 at precisely 1:00 am. He made me put my head in his lap. I couldn't believe it. I was about to die and I didn't have a chance to get my life right. I was going out like this. I actually felt what the millions of women felt before they were found raped and mutilated. I was crying hysterically all while he was taking me to his lair, wherever it was.

I could see the street signs. I kept my eyes on the windshield, looking up while my head was in his lap. I didn't panic. He told me to stop crying. He hated it when they cried. Now that freaked me out! This man does this for fun. So many women were his victim. He had been picking women or boys at random. Surely nothing about me looked like a girl this night. He roamed the streets looking for people to shatter their lives and murder their self esteem. Just to bust a nut. As the car came to a slow creep, he made me get up. He demanded I take off all my clothes.

He made me suck his pissy smelling, none circumcised, disease infected dick. I gagged and wanted to throw up. With the steel to my head, I put my skills to work. I sucked this man's dick like he was my husband. He was very mean, extremely aggressive, and he smelled of straight funk and filth. Then he stuck that nasty motherfucker in me and all while he stroked me he kept that gun to my head. My head continued to hit the window. I kept crying silently and visions of my mother kept surfacing.

Death! I could see blood all over my mother's face. I saw my son without me, my precious child. I was mortified and I felt completely defeated. I needed help.

I started praying. I didn't know if this man wanted to cum and shoot at the same time or what his kinky fetish was. I could tell he was about to bust he grabbed my hair tightly and thrust in me one last hard time. He was finally done. He wouldn't let me put my clothes back on, during the act he promised to let me go. Yet, when he was about to drive off he said, "Put your head back down in my lap." "Fuck you" Jean shouted, "You said you were going to let me go." I was so glad to see her because at this point, my attitude was just kill me!!! When he looked at my face he no longer saw fear, he saw hate.

My daddy always told me never lay down when someone has a gun on you. Shit, you may as well kill yourself. His look startled me into silence. The determination in Jean's eyes didn't fade. He knew that we would now fight to death. Fuck you and your gun. He popped the locks and told me to get out. Then he said, "Walk, don't run, and don't look back." I did just that. When I heard his car go into gear I sped up the pace. I ran stark naked through the alley.

When I hit Fullerton Street, I was less than six blocks from my house. People were honking their horns. All kinds of strays were offering me help. No one was to be trusted. Jean asked. "Where was your knife?" I was always good with a knife. I'd cut many yet never myself. Just to get some cigarettes that were killing me anyway! They could have waited. That's what I got for having my dumb ass out there at that time of night.

To lie down willingly was one thing, but to be made to give it up by gun point was mind boggling. It was the first time I had been raped. I didn't know it wasn't going to be my last. All I could think about were the women that never made it home. I felt their terror. This time I wasn't on a mission of any kind. I had it coming to me or it wouldn't have happened. At least that's how I looked at it. When you live of the world you will be shown nothing but what it has to offer. This kind of stuff will always be bound to happen in the ghetto, in the slums of the city. I felt lost. There was no Jay. He was my god. I didn't know Jesus well enough to know about faith.

Jean always left me hanging; I spent most of my life totally alone with dreams of one day being a star or a successful person of some kind, running something. Experiencing shit that you only see on TV, where you're devastated every week or where anything, tragic is bound to happen at any given time because of your lifestyle is damaging. Knowing that I was brought in this world by two irresponsible drug users and never asked to be here made me feel victimized. I know my children probably felt the same way. My life was doomed since birth. I remember shouting out loud "I HATE YOU!!" to myself.

I made it home and banged on Mr. Ali's door. I was naked, in shock and definitely out of breath. At the site of me, he immediately handed me the blanket he had covered Jamarie with. Thank God my son was asleep. He dialed 911. EMS came and took me to Detroit Receiving Hospital. I hated hospitals and do to this day. It reminds me of jail. You just can't leave if you're admitted; try to leave you will go to jail.

The staff was just as disturbing as the rapist. They picked and probed, took pubic hair from my vaginal area, hair out my head, swabbed my mouth and gave me one big horse pill to take for disease and another one to start an immediate abortion just in case this man got me pregnant. I felt dirty and wanted to kill the man with that infectious dick who left a rank taste in my mouth. They told me not to bathe or brush my teeth. I could still taste him; all I wanted to do was get high. I wanted to think of anything other than that maniac.

Everywhere I went I saw him. He was in the mirror and he was in my eyes every time I sat still. It took a long time to remove his face from my daily activities. I can still see him when I speak of that occurrence. There are things you can't erase no matter how hard you try. It would take a good dose of amnesia to forget. If I could only get high was my thought.

Getting high made me forget about everything but getting high. Plus Jean was close by with her low life ass. She was a rotten piece of shit and she made it clear each passing day, month, and year she didn't give a fuck about me. My tears and fears were for myself defeating behavior!! I knew I was going straight to hell and continued to jump on the first thing smoking to get there. As I look back on the mistakes and the poor choices I made, I didn't care. I could block out things any time I wanted.

The next day I didn't leave the house. I was too scared. I felt like bad luck was coming for me and it did repeatedly. Jean talked about me and I didn't care. Seriously, I was afraid to leave the house. I was afraid of dying. It loomed over me. Hell, I was scared to even go into my own basement. I kept seeing the man's face everywhere. It crept up in the strangest places. I always had to keep doors open. To this day I use the bathroom with the door open.

I can't stand gloom and doom. The rooms in my house have to stay lit up. I was told by my neighbor to start reading the bible. I could never understand it. Too much thee, thou, and people I didn't know and couldn't relate to their problems. Those things happened a long time ago. It just didn't make sense to me. So, why read it? Jean told me it wasn't going to help me anyway. She was right. It didn't help. I stopped reading it.

Jean and her people always said, God Damn, not God Bless. I believe I was cursed, all the way down to my children. Well it was time to do something. I was bored to death. It had been a month since the rape and I knew of a house around the corner that sold drugs. It was time for them to meet us. I had a hundred dollars. Dope houses are never hard to find. I can smell a fiend anywhere. Some of us had a certain look. You could just tell, especially if you look at one's hands. The hands tell it all.

I got dressed. I was ready. Jean and I talked on the way over. My dad kept Jamarie. He knew I needed some time out. My dad had started to settle down from his wicked ways. So sitting his old ass down was cool with him and me too. Nobody knew us on this street. We lived on Clements and the spot was on Grand, directly around the corner from my house. I watched a couple people first before trying to score. Everything seemed to be cool.

There was a time when you couldn't just walk up to anybody's house talking about can I get some drugs? You had to know somebody and you never saw the man either. The real man was never seen. See, everybody had a boss and they owed somebody. That's why I never believed in credit. You would get your ass torn out the frame if you were late. The person you got it from has to now cover your ass to his man and so on and so forth. The game is no joke. It's definitely cut throat and that's putting it mildly. It was never this easy to score. Jean asked, " Are you going to knock or do you want me to?" I wanted to knock because I didn't want her to get ugly, especially at the dope house.

Most dealers solely depend on your money to survive. I know I bought many dealers their homes, cars, and such. Every time you score, you're paying their bills, buying their clothes, and whatever else. Without us they would be useless. Imagine if everyone in the world stopped getting high. The dealer that doesn't have a backup plan, education, or skills, would be in trouble. He's solely dependant on a crack head to show up in order to eat. That's deep but the truth. The dope man used to see me and flag me down. They knew once I got started it was on. I was going to make the money by any means and bring it straight to them.

Before I could knock, a nice looking guy came out. He had long wavy hair. He was mixed with something. He wasn't all black. He had a small handicap. His left hand was smaller than his right. He had a gorgeous smile. He the same kind of hat that Gilligan use to wear on Gilligan's Island.

It was denim with the matching jacket. The guy was extremely bowlegged and had the cutest wrinkles around the corners of his eyes. I said a very cheerful and definitely playful hello. He said, "Damn!!! What's your name?" I almost said Sunshine. I told him my name was Pam. He looked at me and asked if I was sure. We both laughed. I said, "Yup." He asked if I was going in. I responded, "Not without you." That was the start of my relationship with David Green. He had the same drug of choice as my mother and father, heroin.

    In Phase Eight I learned about compassion for another. I never had any until I imagined the many females that never made it home to their families who may have only gone out for a few for food or whatever and some spineless ass hole took it upon himself to take their life.

Phase Nine

David didn't main line. He skinned popped and smoked a little bit of Cocaine. David's grandmother had passed away leaving him a lot of money and he chose to get me high with a great deal of it. We were hanging buddies every day. Jean liked him. She thought he was cool I guess. As long as we were killing ourselves nonstop, she was cool with it. We were together me, David, and of course this bitch Jean was like my arm; just there.

We were so high off the Cocaine I had to calm down. I was so wired I could have lit up the entire Motor City. I actually couldn't talk. I was drooling and my body was jerking. I was not functioning properly. I was showing signs of having a stroke. The dope had a funny cut on it. I had to use sign language to indicate I needed a hit of the heroin. He said, "No, you can't handle this." I continued to jerk and point to his plate that held the only thing that could calm me down at that precise moment. I couldn't stop twitching. My body was in spasms.

My body was moving without my permission. I had to calm down. All I needed was one line. David gave me what looked to be a grain of salt. Jean screamed, "Do it!" I had never been that high. My heart was racing. My eyes were bucked so wide, I felt like someone was prying them open. My chest felt like it was going to explode. I snorted the small amount he held to my nose on a card and I felt absolutely nothing. I don't know what I expected, maybe a miracle of some kind. I managed to ask him when it was going to take effect. His response was for me to relax.

Most heroin addicts I've seen had a high that was mellow, almost like weed but a little more extreme. After a couple of minutes I started getting hot, like someone had place the sun right outside the door. I had to remove my clothes. Beads of sweat were popping of me like grease off frying chicken. I took off all my clothes and instantly I was extremely cold. It was like being naked standing on a block of ice. I had to put on my clothes. Then the sweats came again and then the chills. I was hot and cold all at the same time.

I had been asking David how the drug was going to affect me and no one was prepared for what happened next. I took another hit of the crack assuming it would balance me. Bad idea, the crack along with the heroin hit my stomach. I had never tried heroin before and it didn't mix in my virgin system. I spit up all the drugs and I fell out!!!!! I was dying right in the dope house. I was around the corner from my own home.

I could see Jean. She was smiling and she wouldn't help me. Jean looked like she was fading out herself. I remember she told me how she stood aside and watched my mother walk into her own death. She was watching me die too. Her plan was working.

I felt nothing. I didn't see any bright light, just darkness. I was going to hell. I would die in a place where well known criminals hung and their way of getting rid of a body was to throw it in a dumpster. The man couldn't take me to the hospital.

He would have been in trouble. I was past trouble. I was in grave danger. I actually died. The cold night air and my father's old school techniques saved me.

David went ballistic. He was terrified and uncertain about what to do. Scared as a cat cornered by a dog, he carried my lifeless body home. He put me on the front porch, banged really hard on the door, and ran. I was in a coma for two days. My dad was a former heroin addict; he felt a faint pulse then went to work on me. It was a look he had seen many times. I wondered if my mother ever over dosed. Now dig, the insanity of me trying to put more drugs into my body to balance out; a high I had never experienced or knew how to handle once it took effect. You would think if you survived like I did, you would stop getting high.

Not my dumb ass. I didn't realize the blessing to be alive. I was at home in my bed. I was shocked to be there because I remembered where I had been and who I was with. When I woke up my father was there. He told me how he had to monitor me, how he used ice water to revive me, as well as walk me around half the night.

I took a bath and got dressed. Jean scared the shit out of me, while I was looking in the mirror. She said, "I know you're trying to get rid of me, but you can't. Not this time and not that way. You will always be mine and you will never be able to leave me." She looked me dead in my eyes and said, "Your life is my call, not yours. Now go check that son of a bitch that gave you that top side." For those who don't know, top side is the purest form of heroin on the streets. I could have sworn she was happy but she had another plan for me.

As if programmed I did just what Jean said. We put on our black clothes. David was asleep. Jean had all kinds of ways to make him pay but I chose to wake him with water. There was a cup of it on his side bed table. He rinsed syringes with it. I poured it straight in his nose. He jumped up, tried to catch his breath, and when he saw me he hugged me so quick, tight, and long. He was speaking so fast. He slobbered out the words, "I'm so glad you're here. I thought you were dead."

I was taken aback. We sat together in silence for awhile. It was a time to really think about what this man had just said to me. Jean looked at him long and hard. She wanted to kill him. She said, "Don't believe him. If you had died here, he would have left your ass right here. Trust no one but me." David and I parted ways shortly after that horrible situation. The more I used, the more I learned that drugs changed everything. You're not yourself and because I started so young, I didn't get a chance to find out who I was anyway.

Phase Nine taught me that drugs would ruin my life.

Phase Ten

Most people grow up at home with their parents. They go to school, play with other children, live a normal life, go off to college, graduate, and find out what they enjoy in life. They have a career, get a good job, find a mate, get married, and build from there. I was lost. I had no direction and was scared to death to succeed. I was told I would end up like my mother. I was told I would never amount to anything. My life was like a name scribbled on a sheet of paper dumped in a hat that was picked by the devil himself. It was a life of pain and anguish. I fell for every trap he set. He was determined that my life wouldn't be wholesome or pure.

I honestly have to say that I deserved hell, death, and damnation. I have lain with many men and woman, sometimes two and three at a time. I even laid with family members just to get one more hit of anything. Just so that I could forget my pain and my constant thinking why am I here? I placed myself around undesirable people so I wouldn't be alone. I felt lost. I asked myself where I belonged many times. Something clearly was not right with me. I didn't fit into this world. At that time in my life I saw that dope fiends had a certain look. Their teeth were rotten, hair fucked up, raggedy clothes, and they smelled like shit. At least that's what I thought until I became just like them. The only difference was I was a dressed up garbage can. I looked decent on the outside yet I was jacked up on the inside. My behavior was just like theirs.

People would say, "What are you doing here? You're too pretty, and much too smart to be in this place." I didn't believe them. I never thought I was pretty and to this day I can find everything wrong with me. Anyway, my pattern was the same each time I got high. I couldn't eat. My weight was down to 90 pounds. My face was so sunk in you could see straight through my head. My chest and my back were the same. No matter which way I turned it was flat. My head was the biggest thing on my body. I was killing myself and didn't know it. I now know it was nothing but God. That's why I'm still here. Back then, I just thought I was lucky and slick. I wasn't slick. I was spared.

I had all of my children out of wedlock and always wanted to be married. I don't even know some of their father's names. I have six children. I had to be paid to have my tubes tied.

That's another story. If I wrote my entire life in this book, it would be an encyclopedia.

Phase Ten taught me that I am no better than the next person and that only you can change you.

Phase Eleven

My second child was born in 1992. His name is Martell. I had another crack addicted baby. He was very small and frail. This little soldier was so strong to have survived the abuse I subjected him to. My addiction had progressed dangerously and tremendously fast. It's amazing how each year I found myself in catastrophic situations where coming close to death was the norm. That was insane. I was actually pulling on the pipe when my water broke Martell was coming and nothing not even getting high could keep him from doing just that.

I had asked my cousin Sheree if I could stay with her for thirty days. On the 29th day I had ten thousand dollars. During that month my licks were good and many people were robbed especially the stores. It didn't matter who took a loss I vowed to never be homeless again and I never was! I was pregnant when I moved in my house. It was a cute little house that sat back from the street. I made my money the same as most addicts; I stole for a living.

I was very good at it. I know anything can turn into an addiction. I had a bunch of bad habits and stealing was one of them.

I didn't know who the father of this little boy was. I had sex with a lot of men for money and I had not realized the seriousness of being a parent. I fed and clothed my children. I provided them with a roof but I did not know how to be a parent. There were no hugs, no motherly affection, or soothing conversations that a mom would give her child. Everything about my world was wild, loud, and chaotic. My children lived like me, day to day.

The dope man was my parent so I treated my children pretty much like I was treated. I treated my sons like they were my little brothers. I didn't know what I was doing having these children like that. They suffered but it was definitely not intentionally. I loved them, just not as much as I loved crack. The lifestyle and my line of work did not require having children. Every two or three years, I went to jail and left them behind. I did large amounts of time. These children had no chance at a normal life with their own mother.

I did not realize that I repeated my mother's behavior. I put my children through what she put her children through. My children would experience the same void in life. They needed a mother as well. It was a vicious cycle. Today I know where I went wrong, yet I can't go back and fix this mess of a life I made for them. To be honest, if I had a choice to do it all over again I would have chosen not to be born.

Martell was born November 21st 1992. He really wasn't given a chance. Jean laid another trap for me. I honestly didn't see it coming. I thought I had her pegged, but I didn't. She was sneaky and even though we were together all the time it was still hard to say what she would and would not do. We went to work. It had been three years that I had been free from the last jail sentence. Even though I have been in jail off and on all my life, this time was the hardest.

I went to jail that day leaving Martell and

Jamarie behind for two long, pain staking years. Martell was two weeks old when I went in and two years old when I came home. What was even more jacked up, I had to do it all in the Oakland County Jail. I had so many unresolved cases and warrants in three different counties. They were all felonies. I knew I would be gone for a long time. The Honorable Judge Hilda Gage out of Oakland County verbally thrashed me. She stated I was a menace to society and I have done nothing in my life but commit crimes. I was a career criminal and I should be punished past the guidelines. She looked at me with disgust after giving me one year after another. She told me if she saw me again, she would make sure I would rot in jail.

  I stopped committing crimes in Oakland County. I continued to commit crimes in Wayne County. The court system in Wayne County wasn't as strict. Jamarie had a godmother that was crazy about him. She promised to take care of him until I came home. Martell on the other hand, was a different story. I asked my sister to keep him. She said fine, yet turned around and gave my son to her best friends Kim and Reggie Glasgow. They were her high school buddies well Kim was anyway. I really didn't have a problem with that until it was time for me to come home. I had papers drawn up for temporary guardianship so I could get my son back when I came home.

It didn't go smoothly. The Glasgows jumped on me. They literally kicked my ass about trying to pick up Martell. It had not dawned on me he would think this lady was his mother. If it had to be like that, I would have preferred it be my sister he would love so hard. Keep it in the family. I went over to the Glasgow's. I was excited to see my son. I hadn't seen him in two years. They were expecting me. I wasn't expecting them to kick my ass as if I was caught kidnapping their child.

They beat me and told me I couldn't have my own child back. The papers I had drawn up were stamped and sealed by the Oakland County Sheriff's department. He was rightfully mine and the Glasgows were sent a copy. They had signed and sent them back. Everything was properly handled through the proper channels. This was an outrage.

My son was given to them by my sister temporarily. It was behind my back. Then when I was informed of it, not only had it been done and arranged, I felt like my sister said fuck me. Yet I had no choice but for it to be alright. I was detained big time. You definitely lose your clout when you're locked up. You don't have any rights except to sit your ass down and do the time they gave you and wait on your out date. Simple and plain, when you're locked up, its just you and your thoughts. You think stupid shit like if only, I should have stayed at home, or the classic thought, why? I did this stupid shit. I had all those thoughts.

What's even more fucked up is on the date he was to come back to me, my sister not there to introduce me to these people. She moved out of state. I was formally introduced to the Glasgows while they were beating my ass. I hated my sister for that and a part of me still does. She didn't know then but she knows now. I have been more of a sister to my brothers and sister than they ever have been to me. They still wrongly judge me to this day. They all had their lives together while I was still trying to figure out who the fuck I was. They act as if they never did any wrong ever. They forgot where they came from. It's something I still go to counseling for.

I believe God keeps my siblings shielded from me and my girl, Jean. For sure, Jean keeps a black outfit for all of them for the day of battle. My sister and I don't get along but maybe for an hour in person before there's a heated debate about some shit. She can't handle that I remember about her past. I know what she did to me and her own children back in the day.

There's no unity in my family at all. We have never had a family reunion. Hell, Lonnie and David act like they're better than me and Curtis. We were all raised separately. David and Lonnie lived with the well off. Curtis and I came up off the curb. So of course our views of life are going to be different. That's why Curtis and I get along and

Lonnie and David get along. When we speak to each other in a group we're fake and it is very far and in between. I can't remember the last time we were all in a room at one time. I know it will happen again one day for sure, when one of us dies. They swear it's going to be me first.

    Anyway, I had to get the police to get my son back, along with his birth certificate and my ID. Man it was pandemonium. I couldn't believe it once I got him home. I decided to rent a house on the same block the Glasgow's lived so we could share Martell. Of course that was a process in itself. He thought this couple was his mother and father.

    To me; that's fucked up to have a child believing a lie like that. I could see if I was dead but I was in jail. At least inform the child of the situation to better prepare them for the big bang when I returned. Kids aren't stupid. They know when something's going on. I stalked my children. I may not have said a word to them, but if I wanted to see them, I did.

My fourteen year old found out where I lived and he would sneak to visit me every day after school. Children want to know who their mom is what she's like. Shit I still want to know and I'm 40 years old. I ended up giving my son back to the Glasgows. I loved him that much. He regressed with me he didn't like me or know me. He wouldn't eat for me. He cried all the time. It was a big mess. We went through the Losing Isaiah saga before the movie came out. I had to deal with the consequences of my own actions. I watched another woman raise my son. I have no words for that pain and I'm one who always expresses myself to the fullest.

Today Martell is with my brother Officer David Marshall. He is currently paralyzed from the waist down. I don't know why. My brother and I don't talk. Martell surprised me a couple years ago and called me. He wanted to introduce me to his girl friend. We spoke briefly. When I tried to call my son back I was asked by Mr. Marshall how I got his number. I couldn't tell on my son for fear he would be in trouble for contacting me, so I didn't respond. I was told to never call again. Long story short I deleted the number. To lose a child in any way is heart breaking. I lost all of mine because of my selfish ruthless behavior.

Phase Eleven taught me my family didn't even deserve the title of family.

Phase Twelve

When times got rough instead of relying on God, I turned to Jean. I just simply felt like I had to do what I had to do, no matter what. I didn't have faith and didn't care to know what it was. I had absolutely no patience. I was a thief, a liar, and a con artist. I stole everything. I never bought anything from deodorant to men's hearts. I misused them and anybody else for my financial gain. I trampled over anyone who freely lay in front of me. My beauty won over many. My conversation was award winning. I had the gift of charm that many wished they possessed. I had that quality and perfected it only to scam!!!

My proper diction was shocking, especially to those who found out I had never finished school past the 9th grade. I had what looked to be class and an Ivy League upbringing on the outside. But deep within I was dark and ugly. I was a tyrant. I had a job to do. It was to take you for everything you had, from money, to your spirit and soul. I was not programmed to be kind. I tried to sneak and be nice but Jean always knew. She sabotaged everything positive in me.

A few months of washing away the pain of losing my son to the Glasgows by continuing to get high, I caught another case. This time I was only gone a year, as if that wasn't enough. I stayed in jail so much the officers knew my name on site. Some would say, "Marshall you're back." They knew just where to place me and what detail to assign me. Now that's sad, but so very true.

While in jail I met Karen. She stayed on the phones. A great way to pass time is talking to the outside. I asked her to hook me up with one of the guys over the phone to write. She called her friend and he turned me on to this guy named Darrell Allen. We would talk all the time. He sent me money from time to time. We got cool and made arraignments to connect when I became free and that's precisely what happened.

He was everything he described his self to be. He was 5' 7", very slim, yet muscular, he had the cut of a welter weight, dark skin, big brown eyes, and kind of cute. We went to the motel that same day I came home. We both brought condoms and neither one of us used them. I had been in jail a year and dealt with no one but him. I came up pregnant immediately. This motherfucker said "It ain't mine."

I told on his birthday, August 2nd. He hung up on me. We didn't talk for a few months. I waited because I knew he was the father. I wanted him to feel stupid. He did. My little angel came out looking just like him. His family was supportive, very good to me, and extremely helpful with the baby. I named him Darrel Lamar Allen, II. We call him Little D. Darrel and I had our moments when we were cool. This man never took any shit from me. He was the man and always handled his business. He, of course, like many was good to me. Darrel bought me and my son what was needed and damn near everything we wanted.

Darrel and I would connect periodically sexually. I got pregnant every time. I have three children by him. That knocks down half the mystery of who the children's fathers are. The second child's name is Darius Lawaun Allen, another bundle of sheer joy. My two little boys were very healthy, happy, and loved babies. Darrel would indeed jack me up for getting high. He would do his own investigation on his boys. Checking to make sure I wasn't slipping on my duties as a decent mom. He would put me in check about using, especially around his kids. When I knew he was coming to see them I had to straighten up. I always tried to keep it together. I never left my children on people unless I was in jail.

I made sure they had the best clothes and huge Christmases every year I was home. My children may have known mommy acted a little different, but they never saw me get high. I gave them any and everything to preoccupy them while I used. You simply just can't get high with or around children. People say that nothing's impossible. Bullshit! That's the one thing that is. You can't get high on crack around kids. It's as if they know exactly what you're doing. They nag the fuck out you by calling your name repeatedly. You have already made sure they have been fed, they have TV, toys, everything and as soon as you take a hit here they come! I had to wait until I put them down for the night or use a downer to keep me from looking so spaced out.

I tried for years to hide this shit from my babies. I became totally exposed because I committed another crime, one that will definitely go down in my family history. No one ever did the things I did. It was just unreal, totally unheard of especially to the Fontain and the Johnson's Family. They don't claim me anyway, so it didn't matter.

Phase Twelve taught me that no matter how you try to dress up shit it still stinks.

Phase Thirteen

I was on Michigan's Most Wanted list for kidnapping, auto theft, reckless driving, abandonment and retail fraud. My life as I knew it had disappeared. I went from one bad decision to another. I was on some straight fiend shit. I woke up one day in a decent home with my children and I was homeless on the run before the day was out. I listened to Jean's dumb, uncaring, sorry low life, ass again.

I went shopping at Westland Mall with a customer. We went to get some coats. We were in her mother's van. She was supposed to be on her way to work. She lied to her mother and picked me up instead. Off we went. She had three of her kids and I had three of mine. Even though my children were there this was my job. I needed the work. Surely this customer had the money to pay me. All we had to do is stick to the plan.

We went into the mall. She picked what she wanted and I made the snatch and grab. Two of my children were in her van along with two of hers. We took my son Little D and her little boy into the store with us. I made it out the store and into the parking lot to the van that was parked a ways from the door. It was a good thing Jean told me to grab the car keys from her. Our agreement was to meet at the nearest gas station if we were separated. That was the plan.

I had the secured merchandise. I pulled the van around to the door and waited for her to come out. I couldn't understand what was taking her so long. I stepped out the van to go get her and the children. Before I could get to the mall door there were two white men grabbing the car door and they already had their hands on the merchandise. They said, "Could you come with us?" Jean didn't leave this time. This bitch wanted to get high and nothing was going to stop her. Not even the loss of my child. Jean told me to sit back. She said to the security officers, "Let me turn the car off." They didn't try to physically detain her.

They seemed to be more concerned with the

merchandise. The look on Jean's face was terrifying. She did the unthinkable; she pulled off dragging security as she fled, leaving my son Little D with my customer. We were supposed to meet at the nearest gas station. She never showed. What's worse this bitch lied on me completely. When security couldn't catch us of course they tried to get her.

This girl was not a criminal. She was a nurse. She had never been in trouble a day in her life. She felt like she had so much to lose. Fuck me and the fact that I was doing her a favor. Plus she had to cover her ass with her mother, seeing how it was her mother's van. She was an accomplice to a crime that gives you a fifty-fifty chance. Either you're going to make it home or go to jail. Of course, there's also a chance of getting killed trying to escape while being chased and such.

I drove franticly to Lynn's mom's house to use the phone. I called the mall to find out the whereabouts of the lady and the children. The customer and her child were released. My child was held in custody with the police and they were only going to release him if the mother came forward. They had my name and address. They knew all about me. They were told by my customer, who also said I had stolen her van and kidnapped her kids. She gave my son to the police to free herself. You know I was going to kill this bitch on site

I don't fuck with a motherfucking snitch and definitely not a liar. I dealt with people that held their own. Now I was shattered beyond repair. I couldn't respond to this madness. My head was spinning. Lynn was disgusted. My son was left alone without any familiar faces and this non feeling tyrant said, "Pam, let's get to the house." There weren't any maternal feelings or thoughts of getting my son at that time.

My street was crawling with police. This bitch gave them my address. Hell just my name and my history alone was enough to do a massive man hunt. Kidnapping is a federal offense. Now what do I look like high off crack kidnapping a poor bitches kids? I couldn't even deal with mine when high, let alone somebody else's. I had no choice but to leave this mess up to Jean. How would I tell Little D's father about his son. He was going to kill me.

I thought of all the things I had ever allowed this bitch to put me through this was the most outrageous, dangerous, selfish act ever. People all over my neighborhood knew I had her kids. Jamarie asked me why had I left Little D. I couldn't respond. Anything I said would have been a lie. I had nowhere to go. I was completely tapped of funds and no drugs.

Jean and I argued for the first time. I had never the look I saw in my child's eyes. He looked concerned, scared, and not to mention confused all at the same time. Jean could have cared less. She had to be free and alone. She spotted this bitch's purse on the floor between the seats.

She grabbed at it as if her life depended on it. Jean looked at me and then this bitches kids. She drove to a store on the other side of town. She took her time checking out the contents of the purse.

The children were getting antsy. They needed food and to stretch their little legs. One of her children was four months old. We had no room for a baby that needed undivided attention. I tried to soothe the children without breaking down into tears and falling totally apart.

Jean all of a sudden hollered, "JACK POT!!!!!" She found three hundred dollars and some food stamps, if sold on the street it would be worth two hundred dollars. Also she had a WIC book that had never been used. It would be worth one hundred fifty dollars on the underground. Now it was time to get right. Jean went to the dope house. She told me as she took the first pull off the pipe, "We got to get rid of these kids." I agreed.

By night fall I was crying for my son knowing he was alone and wondering where his mother was. I couldn't relax. Jean saw this mess through a different pair of glasses; her plan to destroy me was coming full circle. I was losing my mind. Getting high was the only thing that allowed me some rest from active thoughts about the events of that morning.

Jean said, "You know where this skank lives, don't you?" We were parked on Hartwell and Chicago. She chose that street to stay informed about the kidnapping. My family lived there. My family tried to warn me about my brother because he was a robocop.

He would definitely take me in. He had arrested me before. We had to keep our distance. Yet, we were right under their noses. That's the last place they would look. Jean thought like the police, just like the police think like the criminals. Jean always stayed not two steps ahead, but a mile ahead. Eventually we would get caught but now we took the risk of dropping her children off at her mom's house.

An elderly looking woman answered the door so fast Jean almost hit her. Jean never spoke. She just started handing her the kids that were in the van. Then this lady said something Jean definitely didn't like. Jean looked up. That's when the lady could see the devil she was dealing with. Jean was leaving the porch when the lady said "What about the van?" Jean turned and looked at her over the rim of the shades she was wearing, those coal black eyes twinkled like approaching darts, and in a tone that was ear shattering, "You're lucky you got these motherfucking kids back, BITCH!!!" The lady watched Jean walk directly to her vehicle and drive away never to be seen again. When she got back to the van, she stared violently at the house for future plans to torment this family later on.

Phase Thirteen totally confirmed I had a serious problem.

Phase Fourteen

Jean was vindictive like that. She would get a fixed idea and she followed it through. Most people say you have to get up early in the morning to pull a fast one on them, with Jean you couldn't even go to bed at night. This bitch never slept. She would lay a trap for your ass. You would definitely regret meeting and/or fucking over her.

Trust me I know. I tried to warn people. When the shit hit the fan they would end up with her standing over them, ready to kill, willing to die on principle. I wondered why she was never afraid of death. Because the bitch was dead already; that's why. Now it was time to put my children in a safe place. I couldn't keep them. They were in horrible danger. This was Jean's life now. It was over for me.

Jean called Big Darrel and told him what happened and that she would be dropping off Darius. But Darrel couldn't be reasoned with or understand me leaving his son. I was an outcast to everyone. This was absurd. He was going to kill me for sure. I had D Morgan drop Darius off with the information to get Little D back. It was December 5th 1998. By December 15th Little D was in the care of big Darrel's mother and father. He currently resides with them today.

In spite of what I did then, this little crumb snatcher sneaks to see me. He loves me harder than life. He is so strong and doesn't care what people say about mommy. He loves to kiss me on my eye lids. I only can thank God for allowing me to find out about Jesus and allowing me another chance with my babies. Well the ones I can see anyway, Big Darrel's family forgave me. We all get along pretty well. It took many years for me to learn that the power of love can withstand anything, even Jean's bitch ass.

It was Jamarie's turn. I called Jeff in Ohio and sent him to his father. I gave him money and packed what I could salvage from my house in the wee hours of the morning when the house wasn't under surveillance. I had to watch the police to make sure I could get in and out of the house where we lived.

I stayed in the van for two months after the mall saga, the whole winter. I was solo with Jean pinching off this snitches money and everything in the van worth selling. Contact with the family was a no no. I lost my entire family in one day from a jacked up decision. My children were scattered around. I had no house, nothing, just completely out of control. There was no glue strong enough to put this mess of a life I made back together. I never once thought to call on JESUS. He was always the answer. I had a nervous breakdown holding a pipe in my hand, parked behind an apartment complex.

I woke up with the dope all over me. I had fallen into a state of delirium. I looked like I had aged 20 years in 24 hours. I wasn't surprised this time. She was right behind me holding me up. I couldn't make it or take it anymore. I was finally broken. Jean was a DIE HARD bitch. She could out last DURACEL, she was that strong. "Bitch you thought you were going out like that." Jean laughed, "Hit this shit, and snap out of it, right now!!!!!! The kids are straight. Fuck that shit in your house. You can get more. Have fun while you can. You're free, dummy".

Jean always rationalized stupid shit and made it sound alright. Here we go again. She didn't want me to have a moment of clarity and do the right thing. She clouded my judgment quickly and captivated my potential to win. I never won with her. I always took a dive. WOW, how real is that? I always lived in the real world and it hurt. I never even laughed at jokes. Nothing was ever funny to me. I stayed totally serious. I got thrilled when danger approached. Disastrous situations made me smile. I always wanted to see the bad guy get away and would be pissed when they got caught. That's insane. DAMN!!!!!

Who am I? Better yet, what am I? How could I have done these unfeeling acts? What kind of mother does that? I was not a mother; I was a monster. I needed to be stomped, kicked, dragged straight to hell, or shot, stabbed, and buried, whatever came first. Guess what? None of that happened. I had to see this destruction. The easy way out was to die or be killed.

I had to be shown what I had done to my babies. GOD knows I am sorry. He kept sparing me. I should have been dead a long time ago. He had a plan for me. I couldn't see this day alive in one piece with all of my limbs working properly and still being beautiful as ever without walking with the Lord. I never thought about how my decisions affected my children. I just hustled and survived. It was all I knew at the time. The pain was blinding. It hurt so bad. I honestly couldn't see the damage I had done and was doing.

As I sat there listening to Jean, I felt a flutter in my stomach and surely I knew what it was. I held my stomach to make sure I felt what I thought I was feeling. It kicked this time. I just sat completely still hoping my stomach was growling. It had been two days since I had eaten and that was the problem. My daughter was hungry. Man, what the hell was I going to do with another baby?

I was tripping. The last person I was with was Big Darrel. I was devastated. I couldn't even get high. I sat in silence for a moment trying to think. This was impossible. I sat in deep thought. I was in hell. "Just go with the flow", said Jean. I did just that.

Phase Fourteen taught me how to live life on the run.

Phase Fifteen

I was still on the run. I started to show a bit. I went to my father to ask for abortion money. He turned me down flat. I truly didn't want another baby and wasn't going to have one. My father was in hospice at the time dying of lung cancer. He said, "Don't kill this one. This is your girl."

It was only a matter of time before I would get caught and I would have to leave her any way. Why put another child through that? I begged my father but he held to his guns. I walked out on him, pissed. He had the money. He died before he could lay eyes on my daughter. Rest his soul. At one time this man was the devil himself. He became a better person when he was dying. He put his kids through a lot of shit. Lloyd Marshall, to my understanding, was not my real father.

I was so fucked up when I found out. This is how I found out. My sister Lonnie and my brother Curtis were with me at my home on Gladstone. We were all in a heated debate about how my father was going to come out of prison doing the same shit and how they had no love for him. To me he was my daddy and I spoke in his defense because he wasn't there to defend himself. This dirty unfeeling skank bitch Lonnie told me he was not my father and that she was his only baby girl.

I blinked out. I ran over to her and knocked fire and sparks from her ass. I knocked her completely out of the chair she was sitting in. Curtis saw her face was bleeding like a running faucet and kicked me down a flight of stairs in my own house. I allowed them both to with me because they were both homeless at the time. I shouted, "GET OUT!!!!" They said, "We ain't going nowhere." I left mentally shattered, physically damaged. I wasn't allowed back in my own home because I defended a man that I thought was my father. Lonnie Marshall will always be my dad to me.

My dad was something else, a cold piece of work, WOW!!! He was so fine. He had light skin, beautiful eyes, and he was smart too. He could answer all those hard ass questions on Jeopardy. He was a lady's man as well. Damn, he was all that and more. All his potential was wasted in prison. All his life he robbed banks and anybody that had money. Hell, he even robbed the famous Prophet Jones!

I remember some thugs he owed some money came to collect when we lived on Clements. These guys came in the door shooting. I was there alone with Jamarie. They slapped me around and straight beat my ass while my son was hollering. I just knew my father was long gone. This motherfucka was hiding in my Murphy bed that was closed.

For those who don't know, a Murphy bed folds into the wall. Mine was in the living room. This particular day it was in the wall with a big heavy HI FI stereo in front of it. My father was able to hide in the wall and pull that HI FI back in place. He listened to me get badly beat for some shit he did. That's the kind of family I had. When they finally left, my father came out. I was dismayed.

Why would this grown ass coward stand in hiding and allow this to happen to his daughter?

I had to think I wasn't his daughter. I hated him for that. Plus, anyone that messes over their mother, surely the next person ain't got nothing coming. He had fucked over his mother. He once threw his mother's, my grandmother's, mink coats out the upstairs window. Lord knows he couldn't walk them pass my grandfather to sell for some blow. I blame him for my mother's death sometimes. She made him her savior. I still have so much pain. I didn't go to his funeral. I was pregnant with my little girl he asked me not to kill.

I was in treatment at Holly Gardens. I was trying to do the right thing for the sake of my father and the little girl I was carrying. My name was the first one signed in the family book at the funeral home. I went the day before to view his body. I was still considered an outcast by the family and no one liked or trusted me either. It didn't matter if I was there or not. I hope he made it to heaven. I have finally forgiven him and loved him dearly in secret. I named my little girl Loyale Rose after him and my mother. OH MY GOD, talk about pretty, she was the most gorgeous baby I had ever seen.

She was dark with slanted eyes and naturally curly hair. Her locks were thick and beautiful. She had the most perfect features. Her nose was cute as a button and her lips were small and perfect. She looked like heaven. Only GOD could make something so perfect. Loyale was so healthy the hospital let me bring her home. I was doing great. I had resolved the abandonment charges. But I was scared to deal with the criminal charges.

I was still on the run. I went to treatment for the wrong reasons. This was my eleventh treatment center. I had a few successful completions for the law or for my family's approval. It was never because I wanted to stop. Jean was still in full control. She would allow me a break which was a part of her plans to further make me look like a fool. To get me to a point where no one will ever believe I could change. Shit, I wondered myself.

I ended up getting caught after the birth of my little goddess. I knew I made the news but not Michigan's Most Wanted. I went to score some drugs and as I entered the spot my boy said, "Damn girl I just saw you on TV." I said, "Yeah right", and handed him the money. I just wanted him to give me my shit so I could go. I had my share of raids and my daughter was in the car. Then he said, "Your name is Pamela Marshall AKA Pamela Green." I stopped dead in my tracks.

See the dope man doesn't know your real name unless he knows you. This fool only knew my name to be PJ. When he called my whole name and my alias I knew he wasn't lying. I was scared to death. People would take money to tell where I was. I hit that lick in a white upscale community and they wanted me caught. It had been months since the kidnapping, six months to be exact.

When I got back in the car Loyale was still asleep. I just stared at her. Somehow I knew it would be one of the last times I would see her and sure as shit, it was. I had been allowed to visit with my boys every two weeks and bring the baby too, so they could get to know each other. Loyale was three months old. We were coming from the family visit with the Wayne County protective services. Even though I had slipped and started using again, no one knew and I still made the visits. But I wasn't fooling the Almighty Father. I still wasn't ready to be a mom. It was time to address the kidnapping charges. Just when you think you have gotten away with something, it's time to think again.

That afternoon my guy at the time pulled into his driveway with me and the baby. As I turned to get out the car a large white man was saying, "Let me get that for you." It was the bounty hunters. There were ten of them. They were everywhere like a swat team. I couldn't run or move. I was flat out caught. Now my guy, D. Morgan, knew my brother very well. He called him while sitting in the Wayne County Jail my second home. I knew I was hit. I didn't even pray. I just laid down and went to sleep. I wasn't there two days before the turnkey called my name, "Marshall! Get up you got a visit." That was nearly impossible. It's a major process before you can get a visit. I knew it had to be the law. It was my brother, Robocop.

The reason for the visit was he wanted to take the baby. I agreed, not knowing for one minute that he would have her thinking I was her aunt. I'll be damned. Of course I didn't deserve my children! I will tell anybody I wasn't fit to have them. Why would you not tell her the truth? What did I ever do to him to make him hate me so much? We used to laugh and play as children and this fool knows firsthand how we lost our family. Why would he further destroy me by having my daughter believe her aunt is her mother and the one that is her real mother is her aunt?

I was sick. I had an incurable disease of addiction. I know he has issues that are unresolved. Maybe he's a little bitter and trying to prove that he can solve the problem. Wrong! Nobody can solve it but GOD. You would have thought I robbed this fool and royally fucked over him.

His fuck ass can't stand the site of me and he treats me like a deadly virus. This little nigga was a wimp. When we were kids I fought for him. I always protected him until we were separated. Now this arrogant bastard thinks he sits on Gods throne alone.

I remember watching the news in prison. I saw two Farmington Hills Police officers tazer the shit out of him. I was concerned at first, but he wouldn't have cared if I was or not. My second thought was it's about time someone kicked his arrogant ass, especially on national TV.

He had arrested and jumped on me in the police department and the other officers watched. The other inmates shouted leave her alone. I had the luxury of seeing it happen. Even he had to stop at a stop sign. They didn't care he was an officer from Detroit. That made it worse. He was in Farmington Hills and as a law official he had to follow the law. I imagine all police officers think they have some kind of diplomatic immunity or something. At the time I hated all police. Sure they had a job to do but they wouldn't have one if it wasn't for people like me.

It was fun out running them when I was younger and pissing them off. Granted I was wrong and I too had to learn life's lessons to appreciate them as God's child. So keep in mind, whoever is reading this, you are no better than the next person. We were all created the same way and will be judged equally. If you have illusions about what I am saying, keep it up, GOD has a way of humbling that ass straight into believing. Trust me, I know firsthand. I have forgiven my brother. We don't know each other at all. I ain't missing nothing. I have a brother that loves me no matter what, His name is JESUS.

This Phase thought me humility.

Phase Sixteen

I ended up doing a year for all those horrible charges. I was never charged with the kidnapping or the stolen car. I was spared again. Hopefully my daughter won't grow up to hate me. However, I'm prepared. I am used to pain of many kinds and one thing I definitely learned dealing with humans is. They are unpredictable. She just may love me. That would be a great read to find out if she will or won't. Either way, time continues to move.

I finished the year and was freed. D. Morgan walked the year down with me and came to see me every week. He sent me money and many beautiful cards and letters. Our time together wasn't fun at all. We had a wild relationship. I now know what we shared wasn't love. He will always be a teacher in my eyes. By watching him I learned what not to do, and that's hide who I am.

I had never seen anything quite like it. Jean despised Dee, and would royally fuck over him in an instant. I cared for this man deeply, however that changed after his many psycho, weird, random acts of abuse came into play. I had been abused all my life by men as if I was targeted for it at birth. This man was completely ashamed of me. No one knew I lived in his house, not his friends, family members, or co-workers.

I had to actually stay in the house. He would lock me in when he went to work. What he didn't know they haven't built a house that I can't get out of, other then jail. If a human made it, a human can break it. I would walk out the front room window while he was at work. The man never gave me a set of keys, as if that was going to stop Jean. Dee and I would get high together. He never wanted me to get high without him. If he caught up with me before I could get home that's when the Mr. Psycho would come out. He was crazy. He blamed me for why he chronically used. I didn't put a gun to his head and say get high with me.

The first time he asked me if he could hit my pipe, I told him no. No friend gives you something to kill you. Dee was persistent. I told him he would have to do it on his own, not by my hand. Jean said, "Turn the fool out. That's more dope for you." I didn't respond. Jean lived in my heart and in the depths of my soul. She knew I was tired of this man putting his hands on me. I wasn't afraid of him, anybody for that matter, I just had nowhere to live at the time. I could deal with anything to keep from sleeping outside again and I do mean anything.

I had just come home. I had no money, no job, I was sick with non addressed mental issues, and felt completely lost every day. I had absolutely nothing to do but hang out. I had been gone awhile and of course Jean would visit every now and then when I was away. What puzzled me the most about her would be her disappearing acts. I would need her in my toughest moments and she would be gone. When she came around, I would somehow feel safe. What tickled me the most about her were her entrances. I never saw her coming.

Jean said, "Let's go around the corner." I immediately said, "Bitch where the hell you been?"

My eyes lit up. I instantly could find all kinds of things to get into. She said, "I told you I don't have time for jail. We would be better off dead then in jail. Fuck this bum. Let's get high. There's some shit in the basement to sell. We don't have to hit a store. Let's just hit him."

We had no money and wanted to get high. We took some antiques out of the basement that belonged to his deceased grandmother. They were very old expensive looking items. I could not believe their worth. We got high everyday for two months from shit out of that basement.

One day, on the low low, when Dee was at work I decided to chill at the spot seeing how I was stuck and couldn't move any way. I was that high. I refused to go into public. I would for sure be in trouble with Dee. I left something open like the living room window and he hated that and the fact I was using without him. With couples that get high together it clearly doesn't work. It's always a fight at the end of the night. You're smoking too slow, his is all gone and he's mad, he doesn't have any more, or you have more than he does. That's when the hiding drugs from each other comes in or sneaking around alone to get high in peace.

When Dee came home and I wasn't there, he came looking as always. He found me, as always. I wasn't predictable. I would find myself in the strangest places. I was subject to be seen anywhere and if you looked hard enough you just might find me in hell, surely that's where I was headed. We were off Schoolcraft and Wyoming. Dee came in his business attire. He worked in the city county building as a mortgage appraiser.

Everybody loved seeing him. They knew he had money. Dee was a secretive person. You wouldn't believe his transformations to keep his using hidden from his family and others. I was sitting in the smoke room. He walked in and asked me for some drugs. By this time they were all gone. That added fuel to the fire that was already blazing in his eyes. He was pissed. "Let's go", he said as if I had called him to come get me. I had no choice. I got up and got in the car. He was silent all the way home, which was right around the corner. As soon as we got out the car Mr. Psycho showed up.

He grabbed me fast and snatched off my new outfit, a denim Capri set I had gotten a while back that I had never worn. Now if anybody knows me, you don't mess with my clothes. He then picked me up and like hurricane Katrina and whipped my small skeleton frame around snatching the breath out my body. He tossed me upside down and through me down so hard he fractured my tail bone. I could only lay there immobile. I couldn't move after being attacked by someone who weighed 200 pounds to my 90.

He then dragged me in the house by my arm. I was locked me down for three days. He stayed home from work purposely to mentally demoralize me, abuse me, hit me at will, and made me sex him. Some might call it rape. When I would drift off to sleep, he would further punish me by keeping me awake interrogating me about who I was with when he was gone. It was the most horrible seventy two hours of my life. On the third day of my punishment, Mr. Morgan wanted to get high. Then we were allowed to get some drugs.

He was a controlling king. If he saw me chewing gum he would place his hand under my bottom lip like you would do a child, for me to spit it into his hand. If he wanted to get his point across in public, if I stepped too far out of line, he would point me in the head with his finger really hard chastising me in a low tone between clinched teeth. Up close and personal, this man had some sick serious vital issues. Shit, I thought I was bad. It was then I received confirmation that insanity is in all walks of life.

Poor abandoned children such as myself weren't the only ones with issues. This man had his mother and his father in the home. He had a decent life. He went to college, had a rewarding career, and he still turned into something that he refused to see. It was just that ugly. What was his excuse for being out cold? Surely, he had a normal upbringing.

Denial is a bad motherfucka. It will cause a

lot of pain. If you can accept that it is what it is, and you can't change anything, especially another human being. Let it be, is my motto. To thy own self be true. I know for fact that when you allow people to be themselves, it's less stressful. When you try to control someone it will wear you out. You did not build this individual; God did. If something is wrong with them, only the person who built them can fix them. Don't worry about the next man. Shit, check your own self.

Some people don't have the courage to change. It's easier for them to show you your flaws. They can't glimpse their own. They are cowards. I never stopped trying. I never stopped hoping for a better way. I begged and pleaded humbly to God for a chance at life on the flip side in peace. Before I could get to that phase in my own life and granted the peace only he brings, I had to really take a look at me and what I really wanted for myself.

So what your mom was killed and your dad wasn't your biological father? There's some stranger walking around the earth somewhere who's really your father. So what you lost your kids? So what you were a crack head? So what the dope man raised you? So what your immediate family black balled you? So what you fucked your life up? GET OVER IT and keep it moving. Those are the changes one can only make for themselves. I learned it the hard way. But by George, I got it and in a nick of time too. I have acceptance that I may have not had the best past and only I, with God, will have a wonderful present and future. I'm strong and willing, which is why I am winning today.

Phase Sixteen taught me we all have problems.

Phase Seventeen

Now, back to this fool, we left the house go back on Kentucky to score drugs. Normally, we would go home, but this time we sat at the trap and got high for hours. I guess he called his self making up for the abuse. Dee was cool with the little dope men in the area. They all trusted him. He would pay on time so credit was never a problem. After the funds were depleted, he gave me the cue to leave him alone with the dealer. Jean said, "Are you ready? Here is your chance to get away from him. Aren't you tired of getting your ass whipped by this big yellow asshole?" I was. She said, "Let me handle this one."

Jean was through with Mr. Psycho. She was the hog with the big balls. I wondered how we would get away. Jean told me not to get high anymore. She knew he was going to fight me that night. I used my skills my daddy taught me years ago. I waited quietly for him to finish the deal. We were going back to his house, my prison. He handed the car keys to me and said, "Wait in the car." He assumed I would cooperate. When he went across the street to get more drugs, Jean snatched the car keys from me, laughing as usual.

I had to brace myself. Shit, it was a shock to me. This bitch would do some of the wildest shit. But she was my girl and it was time to go. She placed the keys in the ignition calmly. She started up the Grey Intrepid and with no hesitation put it in gear, reverse. She didn't want to take a chance on him trying to stop the car. He was standing roughly a hundred feet from where the car was parked. She backed up fast and straight to Schoolcraft, not looking right or left. We were headed towards freedom from the daily violence. We were driving fast but we never once had any concern about the police. We were running out of sheer desperation. We sped through a few lights. My heart was racing. Jean looked at me and said, "Bitch that was like taking candy from a baby."

Jean and I went to the twenty four hour Meijer's in Livonia to get some time in on the clock. We had no money and since we were driving that would be easy. We were successful. It was party time for three days. This man had tormented me. He had taken the weekend to do his dirt to me. Well the weekend was over. He would definitely need the car. Yet doing the right thing never crossed my mind. The only thing to do was to keep driving and we did just that.

The days came and went. I held on to the little Grey Intrepid. Jean and I hung like wet clothes. It was summer, definitely hot. I will never forget it was on a Monday he had to be at work. Jean didn't give a rat's ass. We were driving in our neighborhood, bending the corner from Meyers and Grand River. We ran smack dab into my long lost buddy, Battle Cat. I called her Battle Cat because this girl could kick a man's ass. Jean called her Daisy Duke.

She was the only girl I knew on the stroll had the balls to wear Daisy Dukes. She had a dynamic shape like one of Luke's girls. She wore the shit out of those shorts. Jean's nasty ass liked them and her for that matter. This bitch was a crazy motherfucka and I loved it because she was real. She was standing on the corner of Plymouth and Steel in front of a gate combing her hair, styling it like never before as if she was looking in a mirror.

Jean said, "Look at this fool standing on the corner doing her hair." I laughed, "That's my girl Daisy. We met in jail." Battle Cat was a money getting hoe. S he always tricked the tricks. They never got the pussy and she always got paid. As we pulled up, I saw this fool had a mirror jimmied in the fence. Jean said, "DAMN baby you working!" Duke whipped around and screamed at the site of us. We were a site for sore eyes. She needed a ride and we were riding. We were all happy to see each other, screaming loud, out cold statements in Ebonics and really ready to get high.

Battle Cat always had drugs. She stayed supplied. This bitch was nothing to play with. When she smoked her dope, people really should have been scared to death to fuck with this wretched bitch, not me. This was one of my real buddies. We continued our friendship from jail on to the streets.

This girl was like Platinum, different from gold or silver. She was a hot commodity. If you could afford her, you had some loot, I'll just say that. She knew Jean liked her like that and never gave her any action.

We headed toward West Chicago with low funds and big talk. It had been a while since we kicked it. We stayed friends regardless of how different our lives were. Battle Cat was a prostitute. Pam was a scam artist by every definition of the word. Some people could see Jean for what she really was but most had no clue. Battle Cat she thought she was always dealing with Pam, but she wasn't. What was about to happen didn't have anything to do with me. I personally could never kill anyone. Jean was the devil's side kick. That unfeeling bitch could kill just because she was bitter and it was D Morgan's turn for all the shit he put us through.

Jean said, "HAAAAY Bitch!!!! What up? Give me a hit." Battle Cat reached in her wig and pulled out all the paraphernalia you would need for a blast from the past for that ass. We got high. This dope was speedy. I was straight trippin'. Daisy and I stayed in the same neighborhood. My line of work was very different from hers so we didn't see each other much, but whenever we did, we had fun. It was 11a.m. It had been three days that I had this car. We had fun and partied the entire time, non-stop. We turned the vehicle off maybe once or twice. Jean said it was best to keep gas and keep it running. By it not being ours, we didn't want it unattended it would be hard for anyone to retrieve it from us while it was running".

Anyway we headed up the road to go to the liquor store to get us some kick ass Cisco. That was our dumb ghetto ass drink back then. It would knock us down to the ground, once the crack wore off. We all tried to stay high as the sky. We pulled up on West Chicago and Sorrento, one of the hottest areas in the Motor City and parked in front of the store. I remember it being hot that early in the morning, damn near 80 degrees.

People were everywhere. There were two

nursing homes, a Laundromat, a car wash, two apartment buildings, the neighborhood bar, a gas station and tire shop all in the area. The hood was getting the day started. People were doing laundry, getting their cars washed, senior citizens taking their morning walks, children are out playing on the stoops of their apartments, nurses on their lunch break and this dumb bitch decides to drag Dee down the street at top speed in broad day light in front of hundreds of witnesses.

She was trying to prevent him from retrieving his car that was rightfully his to have. Everything happened so fast. I didn't see him coming but Jean did. Battle Cat went into the store to get the drinks. Suddenly a yellow cab pulled up in front of us. To my surprise it was Dee, I had the window down. He approached the vehicle and snatched open the door. He tried to push Jean over and drive off with us. Jean said, "No can do" and pulled off dragging him down the street. The door was swinging in and out as he was holding on, yanking him back and forth. One arm was in the car trying desperately to hold onto the steering wheel. You would have thought he was trying to take my car the way she fought him about taking his own car back. That's a lot of nerve.

Then the unthinkable happened. There was an oncoming car. Jean didn't care she kept going, smashing him in between his car and the other vehicle. People screamed and shouted, "OH MY GOD!!! She's killing him." You could smell rubber burning. I thought it was from the tires; it was from his shoes. Jean was dragging him at top speed. She was trying to kill him and he no doubt was injured. I could hear Battle Cat yelling at the top of her lungs, "Bitch stop! You're killing him."

Jean was a demonic force that couldn't be tamed. It was wild, loose, and extremely hazardous to one's health. She didn't care that there were people watching, children crying, and elderly people in shock hoping there pacemakers didn't give out. It was something rarely seen, if ever, other than on television. Somehow he developed the strength to get him in the car. When he stopped the car Jean calmly got out. She never said a word to him. She didn't ask if he was okay or check him for any injuries. She walked over to the little white Escort and said to the driver, "I don't know how the insurance thing goes but you can talk to him." She pointed in Dee's direction.

The driver of the Escort had no words. His face was as if he saw the devil in living color. Jean turned on her heel and walked slowly to where Battle Cat was standing with her hand over her mouth. People were looking at us with sheer terror in their eyes and every last one of them could ID us for attempted murder. The only thing on Jean's mind was that ten dollars burning a hole in her pocket. She couldn't wait to get to the little dealer up the block.

He sold the biggest nickels in the world. We copped and sat in the field. We got high as the cost of living and the events of that morning were placed deep in the crevices of my mind. That means we didn't give a fuck. Every time I sat down, I had to sit slowly from the injuries Dee inflicted on me. Of course, I was homeless again. I wasn't really concerned where I was going. I could always flop at my cousin Tyrone's house. We called him Red because he was light skinned with freckles. He looked like the Marshall men; very attractive, a ladies man like the rest of them. Red had a lady friend who frequented his apartment and she was very jealous of our relationship. We are that close, even to this day. Red is close to Jean too.

He is one of the few that can tolerate her. It's just as vicious as torrential rain when the two of them argue. When they fall out, they don't stay out. That's Jean's boy. In the last few years Red straightened up his life to get his daughter. Jean had to respect the fact that her old running buddy hung up his horns. Jean's horns were permanent, she had no intentions on hanging them up, ever!!! Jean would have to be killed. She didn't care about anyone's feelings. Her heart was made of cement and it beat for no one but her.

So on this particular day, Red was busy. I chose to hang out on the family block and visit my cousin Sheree. Sometimes my cousin tripped off the crack high and put everybody out. She would put her own children out from time to time when she didn't want to be bothered. If her kids had nothing coming then you know no one else did.

So I chilled there with her wild ass for a few. We got high for a couple hours. When I ran out of drugs something had to be done. It was time for a victim. It was about five in the morning when we left my aunt's house. We went toward Plymouth where the hoes hung out. It was the perfect place to catch one. I never made it off the block before someone was speaking saying hey sis. It was a regular hoe named Angie.

She had been shot in the face by a trick. She had a couple bolts and screws stuck in her face. She still had her ass out there making her money. That's what dope fiends do. They are like the Energizer bunny. We keep going and going, no matter what. Anyway, the cat she was riding with got one look at me and decided he didn't want her services any longer. He paid her to get out. He paid me to just ride. He propositioned me for a hundred dollars. I took him up on his offer. There was something different about him that pulled me into saying yes. I wanted to have sex with him. He was very cute and he looked unreal to be creeping the stroll in the wee hours of the morning.

He was extremely clean. His hands were perfectly manicured. His cologne was just right. You could tell it was expensive. He had beautiful hair and caramel skin like he was wearing make-up. His teeth were so pretty like on a Colgate commercial. It was too good to be true. He had to be the police. He wasn't. He drove a bus. This man in this big beautiful truck had me going. I was 33 and had enough experience with men to know he wasn't lying. He really wanted some pussy and I really wanted to give it to him.

We made love in his truck without any protection and it was so good. He gave me the hundred plus what he gave me to just ride which was forty dollars. He told me if I ever needed him stand on the corner of Schaefer and Grand River. He gave me the days on a sheet of paper and shared that he was married. I could tell he was a married man and that something was missing in his marriage to cause him to seek love from strangers in the street.

At any given moment you could be facing Doctor Jekyll and Mr. Hyde, you just never know. This ride wasn't so bad and even if it turned out to be a nightmare, I was alright with the decision I made. I learned if you knew that the consequences of your actions were going to be jacked up, you also had to know it would be you who had to deal with them.
I had placed myself in a compromising situation. I could have caught a horrible disease and risked another pregnancy. That, I clearly could have gone without. I know I must be crazy. As sure as there is a GOD, I ended up pregnant. There were a few men who could have been the father. The father wasn't a concern for me, getting high was.

I couldn't imagine being homeless again with another child, so I asked Tyrone if I could stay with him for awhile. As usual, the door was open.

I often said to him that I had to stop smoking this shit and get my life together. His response to me was I will always be here for you and he has. Thank you Tyrone. I love you.

Now let me tell you about Red. He was a heroin addict. He put that down many years ago, but this red bastard could out smoke Bob Marley. As a matter of fact, if he didn't have his weed, you and everybody in his way would have a bad day.

So on this day in June, we were sitting in his apartment using our own drugs. I was four months pregnant. I really started having thoughts about having all these crack babies as well as having warrants out for my arrest everywhere.

The one I wanted handled was the probation violation out of Frank Murphy Hall of Justice. I had a friend help me out. He was a court clerk. I asked him my chances if I came into court. Would I go to jail? He said, "No. Come on down here. Get this old case over with." He promised me I could get it done without going to jail. I caught the bus downtown carrying my last child in my belly to clear up something that could hurt my chances of having any kind of life with my baby. I was a pregnant fugitive walking into a court house loaded with stolen merchandise, drugs and paraphernalia.

When we got to the court house, I was just coming down off a blast. I signed in and took a seat. I nodded to my friend who was the court clerk. I was happy that this violation would be squashed and I could go home. There's nothing like going in a room and not coming back out. It's never easy turning yourself into the authorities. I found myself doing it a lot. I never stopped trying to get it together. I know I am a strong woman. I just didn't know I would have to have strength to endure what was about to happen next. That's why you don't plan anything. God has a plan for all of us and He had one for me in this court room.

I was sitting there trying not to look high especially since I was pregnant. Jean tapped me on the shoulder and said, "Let's go." I didn't respond. I continued to sit there. I always ran from the law and was tired of it. I could only run so far and only hide for so long. Turning myself in would definitely lighten my sentence if given one. When the bailiff walked in and said all rise I was expecting to see cut loose a frail little white man that wore cute little bowties and small wire rimmed glasses.

Instead a beautiful young black sista enters the court room, Judge Vonda Evans. I thought she was so pretty. She had a gorgeous hair cut with sass and pizzazz. Most judges are old as time, wear glasses and look over the rims at you before they send you to hell. That's what jail is, hell. She did a few cases before mine. When my file came up they read my case number, which lets you know it's your turn. However I was told I wasn't going to jail and I know the law, as many times I faced a judge. If someone promises you freedom you won't go to jail. That's why they ask if anyone made you any promises.

Once they read off the charge, she looked at me. Hell, it seemed like she looked through me and asked if I was pregnant. Your file has everything you've ever done or shall I say got caught doing. She knew I was a career criminal with a lengthy track record of drug abuse. The woman I had been admiring from the start blazed me, publicly humiliated me, used words short of a cursing me out. My high was blown for real. She asked, "Miss Marshall can you drop clean for me now?" I always told the truth. I said, "No ma'am." I lied when asked the last time I used.

      I told her yesterday. I wasn't going to tell her twenty minutes ago. She looked at me with hatred for anyone who abused themselves and children. She told me that I was a poor excuse of a mother. She said, "You may as well hand feed your baby poison. I am going to make sure that this child you're carrying is not going to be abused any further." I was directed straight to the back where there is a hallway leading to a tunnel that takes you straight to jail. I was going to be in more trouble once the female guard searched me. Talk about a bad day! I was placed in a holding tank.

I sat down and immediately started crying. I was exhausted but my run was not over. I could tell. I felt it. The locks turned and it was the guard who locked me down. He said that the judge wanted to see me again. Vonda Evans by law couldn't lock me up. I had been promised no jail time. She said, "Okay Miss Marshall you are on my case load."

She was trying to save my child's life. She said, "Be back here on July 6th in treatment and clean or you will have your child in Scott Correctional Facility for women." I was so happy because I was about to finish where me and Red left off, using the rest of my dope. Jean kept saying to me, "That bitch ain't playing with you Pam." She really wasn't.

I was afraid of her. The sista meant business and all of us knew it. Red and Jean were silent. I should have been but I couldn't be quiet. I would have started thinking. I wanted to be mad at this lady for helping me. Red told me when they were taking me to the back that the clerk jumped up and said something to her for her to turn right back around and release me. That had to be when my friend the clerk told her that he promised me no jail time.

I went to Red's house and got high one last time and then I went into treatment. I chose Positive Images treatment center on East Grand Boulevard. It was a nice place and the facilitators were great. They cared about me. It was more than just a center; it was home and I loved it there. The food was awesome. I gained weight quickly. They gave me a little extra love because for awhile I was the only one there that was pregnant. It seemed like there was always someone who could see in me what I could never see in myself. Some would call it favoritism, however the staff didn't make it easy for me. You had to want it and at the time I truly did. I did very well.

Dee found out I was in treatment and came to see me. He even came to get me on some of my weekend passes. He thought that the baby could possibly be his, but it wasn't. Dee did not want me back in his life. He had started a new life of his own and was content with where he was in his life. He would later regret leaving me hanging again. He filled my head with false promises that once I completed treatment I could go back home with him.

He lied to me and I had to be alright with the second step of my program. Community placement was like a recovery house. I had my share of bunkies and just wanted to go home. Anybody's home was better than sharing a house with a bunch of women, who were just like me or worse. I know for a fact that there are people who have more serious issues then I do and I never minimize another's.

I got to the point where I loved being clean and sober. I went to NA meetings. My old wounds had started to heal. I had begun addressing some of those issues that needed to be addressed. I started going to regular meetings, where the people were happy to see me on a regular basis and were concerned about my sobriety.

I was told many times how I wasn't going to amount to anything. That I would never change. The old wounds that started to heal from the many years of abuse were continuously reopened by the enemy. It's a shame when the wound is open and a heartless miserable person continues to pour salt in it with the negative talk. Those who said negative things to me are still my motivation. Thank you.

I was pregnant with my 6th and last child. I went to the high risk prenatal unit at Hutzel Hospital. I was considered to be a high risk pregnancy and had to be monitored twice a week. On Thursdays, the females of Positive Images had to go to this NA meeting on Baldwin not too far from the placement. All of us girls could not wait to get out and interact with people that were clean and had their lives together.

I would have to leave the meeting early to catch the bus or ask someone from the meeting for a ride because I had to go to prenatal appointments. I asked the man sitting next to me, Mr. King. He was the finest guy at that meeting. He had alluring light brown eyes, like almonds with long eye lashes. He had a beautiful smile and had a winning personality to go with it. I heard him share at the meeting and for sure this was the man for me.

I remember staring at him and saying to myself he sure looks good. He dressed nice and smelled even better. I wondered if he had a girlfriend. I was still single. Unfortunately there was not a day that went by that Jay didn't cross my mind. What we had was just a stack of horrible memories, stored away to never surface again. Life was easier without him. It seemed I couldn't find true happiness. He tainted my views and opinions about men. I blamed every man for his bullshit. Yet Mr. King was a real man. I could feel it and he was.

Phase Seventeen taught me how it felt to be free from active addiction.

Phase Eighteen

Mr. King agreed to take me to my appointment. We had gotten to know a little bit about each other and we exchanged numbers. I wasn't supposed to be smoking cigarettes but I asked him for one. He gave me half of what he had and dropped me off. Mr. King was driving a cute little truck, a KIA sport. It was burgundy, one of my favorite colors.

Mr. King never judged me. Hell he had a powerful story to tell too. I guess we all do. My body continued to heal. My time at the center had come to an end. I had a very successful completion. I went on to the sobriety house owned by a dear friend of mine, Sandy Karnes. This woman was awesome and very successful. She treated people fairly. She would break her leg off and give it to you if you needed it. She helped save my life many times. Thank you Sandy.

I had completed all my phases of treatment. I had to see Vonda Evans again. I showed up as a walk in. Someone forgot to give me a return date. After she heard all her cases she looked at me and said, "Can I help you Miss?" I stood and reminded her who I was. She stared. I was clean and I could drop for her too. I had done the grown up thing; I turned myself in, again. This time I had my act together. She stated that she was proud of me.

After our conversation, she closed my case. I was free again and able to move forward. Thank you your honor. I left the court house ready to have my own place. I was tired of the lock up set. I was tired of getting permission to do this and that. I wanted total freedom. I could never deal with peoples rules. I had to have my own and Mr. King gave me a chance. We were really a great couple. We enjoyed some of the same things.

He put me in his home, a very cute little duplex on Outer Drive. He took very good care of me. He had a great job working for the city of Detroit. He spoiled me when he could. He was a faithful man, very loving, and compassionate. At that time he was really the best man I had ever dealt with. I was so huge, Mr. King wouldn't have sex with me. He was scared he was going to hurt the baby even though the doctor said that sex would be good for the baby to induce labor. My child was overdue. She was due in August, it was now September.

I had an open protective service case because I had developed a history of neglect. For the safety of the child an immediate investigation was requested by the Hospital. I had to tell the truth in order to get the proper care. They baby's first stool would help make the decision. Everything I ever consumed while carrying her even the drugs would be in that stool.

GOD continued to show me favor. Her first stool was dumped in me during the delivery. The Doctors had to stop the birth to wash it out. The next stool was clean. On September 11, 2002, the last child I would ever have was born. I remember getting up in the middle of the night. I thought I had to use the bathroom.

It had been a long time since I had a baby. I forgot about the pressure from the baby pushing their way out. It was time. My precious heart was coming. I woke up Mr. King and we went to the Hospital. Now this man was heaven sent. He stood by my side and assisted in the delivery. Thinking back I had all my children alone. None of the fathers were there. Even though Mr. King was not this child's father, he was my man and he represented that to the fullest extent of the word. He cut the umbilical cord and dig this, he took full responsibility for her. He gave her his last name. Malika Nakiya King was destined to be with me, and GOD knows I wanted her.

I loved her so much. The three of us were a family for a long time until my son came home. Mr. King did the best he could. I ended up walking away from the relationship for my son. I have to leave that alone. It's another story. I have had to deal head on with the reality of very painful moments while writing this book. I am the first to admit I have not addressed a lot of my painful issues. One day at a time, right?

I still didn't have a clue on how to be a parent. Sure, I fed them. I provided hugs and kisses but how do you really parent a child? Sure, I taught them how to cross the street, to keep away from the stove, and such, but with my low self esteem and constant fears I honestly had no guide how to raise them. I had never finished school, so by all means, don't bring me any home work. I still have a fear of math, which is why I have not gotten my own diploma yet. Also, Jean was in my head all the time telling me to do stupid shit, especially when things went wrong.

I spoke to my children like they were my little brothers. That is why I still don't get respect from them. I can only blame myself for this. I talked to them like they were my friends, and I would curse them out like people on the street when they pissed me off. It's funny with children, no matter how badly you treat them they still want to be with you. I am getting better and I go to therapy for a lot of things. I am a work in progress.

I remember asking my oldest son Jamarie if he hated me. His response was no, but his actions showed differently. I put him through hell, all of them, for that matter. They needed a mother's love and I was looking for the same thing. I was a child in a grown woman's body. I was very immature and really didn't need any children. The one person I don't lie to is me. I never have and never will. When my oldest son came running to me so did his troubles.

Protective Services had came back into play. My son had gotten into so much shit. He went to jail and it put a lot of strain on my relationship with Mr. King. The Detroit Police Department sent him to juvenile and then protective services came after me and my daughter. I was granted custody of him again. I fled with my baby. I couldn't stand another loss. This time I wasn't getting high. I was sober. I had a job working at Bing Steel.

I had a lovely apartment and I was a crossing guard. Life was pretty good. I was just learning how to be a citizen and here comes trouble.

Jean helped walk it in my front door. Again you have to be okay with the decisions you make. I knew my son was too much of a challenge for me. I wasn't prepared for him mentally. He worked on me and he played on my guilt for not being in his life. It was crazy. I couldn't handle it, none of it. I turned to my old comfort. Dope man here I come.

I received a card in the mail from a case worker. She may have wanted to take my little girl from me. I fell off the face of the earth.

I quit my job. I packed my shit and lived in my car for four months. Those were hard times. Falling back into the street life that last time was definitely not easy. I had been clean a couple years with a slip or two, but nothing serious. The one and only person who stood by me was my Aunt Nina Mae Yarbrough. None of my family offered me a place to stay. People still treated me like I gave them VD, especially my brother. My aunt would look at me with the deepest sorrow in her eyes. She only wanted me to do the right things. The life I constantly lived was going to end tragically.

I saw death for myself every day. I slept in the car under my aunt's bedroom window. No matter where I went through the night on my many capers, from robbery to shopping and anything that walked hand in hand with the devil, at 9:00am I was back with food and whatever my aunt needed. It wasn't unusual for me to bring her a mink coat periodically for helping me. I paid her with a mink just to use her car. My licks provided me with serious cash so to give my aunt a mink coat was nothing. My daughter and I were like Thelma and Louise. I rode around committing crimes with a three year old little girl. Even though I kept her happy, fed, and of course well dressed, I had to be stopped. I always talked real to her. I spoke to her as if she were my age. We would take our baths on the side of my aunt's house.

To her it was fun. It was summer. Hell, she thought it was just playing in the water. I got dressed from the trunk of my car every day. I wasn't ashamed of my current circumstances. I always stayed real. What others thought of me didn't matter then and it doesn't now.

    This was a dangerous time. I had fallen off the face of the earth. I couldn't be contacted. I didn't have a mailing address. I was non-existant, living in a red escort without valid plates, just winging it, scared protective services was going to take the only child I had left. I had to really be careful. My brothers would lurk around, both of them. I was asleep in the car and could feel a pair of eyes willing me to wake up. My favorite brother, Curtis was standing there looking terrified. He always did. He was scared for me, and on the real he is to this day. I was staying on the family block. My cousin Sherrie and I would hang all the time. She would always ask Jean, "W hat you got good for the head?" Sherrie was one of Jean's favorite cousins. This loose screw knew, if nothing else, I always had money or access.

    I said, "Come on bitch. Let's ride." We got as high as you could possibly get. We stayed in the car for at least ten hours just smoking and riding. The car was one of my favorite places to use. I always had car related tragedies without having accidents. Like the time my cousin and I had Dee's car. This fool saw us driving past him. He ran across Plymouth and jumped on the trunk of the car to dive straight into the sun roof to get it back. We were both looking good and stupid at each other. We laugh about that stupid shit now.

       Phase Eighteen taught me that everything changes.

Phase Nineteen

I have had so many adventures that I decided to keep under wraps for the sake of incriminating myself. As the night went into morning we were about to run out of gas. The car was a stick shift so just a few dollars would be cool. Jean decided to sit at the gas station for a few. A victim would arrive sooner or later. This station on Meyers and Joy road was the hottest one in the area. Somebody would help us soon. Sure as shit, this little bum comes bouncing around the corner bobbing his head in a world of his own, rapping to a beat only he could hear.

Jean went into the gas station behind this character. We were in distress. "What's up with you and your girl?" he asked. I said. "Shit, broke, out of gas, and want some crack." To my surprise he had everything we needed. He gave us gas, cigarettes, and plenty of dope. This guy was about 25 years old and looked like a derelict. He wasn't a dealer. He was a user. To me, he was too young to be on crack. My thought was if you started using drugs in the new millennium then you had to be the dumbest person in the world. Had I known it was going to corrupt my mind and destroy my life even further than it already was, I wouldn't have ever tried it.

This drug is nothing nice. This shit not only causes self destruction, it destroys everyone and everything around you. Anything I touched turned to shit.

After we got the gas and smokes, we went to my aunt's house and sat in the drive way. We sat at her glass table under the umbrella as if we were having a picnic until the sun came up. I thought he was very nice. He didn't try to hit on us or proposition us for sex. I guess we all just needed a peace of mind that morning to get high. It's so chaotic trying to get high. I dropped him off that afternoon after I went to work. For those who haven't caught on, my job was shoplifting every single day; sometimes twice a day.

Sherrie cooked some food on the grill. We came back on jam as usual. I asked Sherrie to ride with me. We went to find the guy. I wanted to show my appreciation to him for getting us straight. When we first saw him, he was a bum. Now he looked so damn good. He looked like the actor Larenz Tate. He was wearing a fitted wife beater that revealed his six pack. His muscles were bulging and he had the prettiest lips and teeth. It was totally obvious I was interested. The urge to lay with him was strong and after having so many men, that didn't happen often.

  I gave him a plate of food, a couple dollars, and a crack rock. We became hanging buddies. He was just too young and he acted like it too. He was a hustling little guy. He had big heart and we worked well together until we had sex. See, you can't sleep with everybody, especially people you work with, no matter what kind of work you do it seems to always get in the way.

  We were a couple for a while, through the good the bad and the ugly. We have done so many things that only Bonnie and Clyde could identify with. We were often separated because of our many visits to jail; sometimes separate, sometimes together. When we were together it was the best. I had made this little guy my savior just like the others. He had taken care of my little family. He bought me a car and a nice home paid up for a year. He had real love for Malika. She called him Daddy Lex. He worked very hard to feed us. This boy was a man to me.

Our challenges were because of his friends and family. They ran this one particular block. The people on his block couldn't stand me and they were not friendly. Even though I was his girl, I had to earn my respect. I earned mine. I had been robbed by one of the thugs on the block, I still came back. After being shot at on the block, I still came back. After multiple attempts to scare me away, I still came back.

Jean was not a scary bitch. if she wasn't in a body bag she could not be removed. Lex knew Jean, he had never met me. Lex and Jean went on many capers together. On this particular night we both had stolen cars. Malika was asleep in the back of the one I was driving. This was the lick of the century for us if it was done right.

We had broken into an after hour joint that was on jam every weekend. We always wanted to get inside. We knew that the people running it had it going on. There were always a lot of traffic and cars parked outside. We knew it was a lot of money in there or merchandise. On this night, after many failed attempts at trying to find the perfect victim we decided to call it a night and take the baby home. As we were driving down the street we saw the owner of the after hour spot leave.

We stopped at the light to talk about it. We were excited. Our gloom and doom was over. This would be easy. He parked around the corner, I kept my car in view close to the corner incase my baby woke up. This fool takes a brick and busted a window in the back of the house. There was a set of bars holding us up. We measured the distance from the window sill to the beginning of the bars. He could fit. He actually started going through the window, but that six pack got in the way. Jean pushed him through scraping skin off his chest area.

Once inside, we checked the house before taking anything. He went upstairs. I stayed on the middle floor looking in the closets taking everything to one area for transport. All of a sudden Lex came flying down the steps like a jet. All you could see was his smoke. Someone was in the house. I dropped everything and we ran straight out the front door. He told me there was a man upstairs sleep. Now if this person slept through the window breaking and the traveling through the house he may have been drunk or dead. Jean said, "Let's go back." This time I parked on the grass. We robbed these people blind. Our cars were filled with merchandise from their home.

I had a family to feed and provide for. This job would take us through for a few days. Our time together was an adventure. Our jobs were very hard and extremely dangerous. We trusted each other. Bonnie and Clyde robbed banks. We robbed innocent people. Had we trusted in GOD, like I do now, those things wouldn't have happened. We paid the price for our greed and wild sporadic acts of violence.

We stole a whole house. We just moved in the place. It had sat vacant for a long time and we were homeless. We bullied our way everywhere we went, we were outrageous. We didn't have respect for anyone, and nobody fucked with us either. Before we were separated for the last time we had a serious adventure that let Lex know who really wore the pants in this relationship.

It was four o'clock in the morning. I can't remember the month but it was summer. The baby and I were in the house sleeping. My cousin came to see me the night before. This ghetto old lady walked with a cane and carried a pistol every where she went. She spent the night. Lex came in waking me up at four in the morning. The dope man wanted a refrigerator. Hell, we didn't even have one. He needed my help and as usual I got up to help him. We left the baby with my cousin and off we went. We went to this abandoned house to steal a refrigerator in a stolen car to take a few blocks to the dope man for thirty punk ass dollars!

Jean would transform in a blink of an eye, especially when she got pissed. It was like a demon force that lived deep within me: I was even scared of myself when I got angry. On the way over to the dealer's spot we discussed the price. Lex and I were different in the get high department. That NIGGA could out smoke Richard Pryor. I was getting old and slowing down was starting to be an option. I didn't just want dope. We needed cash so we could have food. I couldn't watch my little girl ever go without. I would do anything for her no matter who had to suffer for it.

We got to Crypt's place. He was tripping because the refrigerator wasn't cleaned out. Hell, it didn't even work. Just as long as the light came on we were home free. Crypt didn't want to pay us until it was cleaned out. Jean lost her mind for sure. I got up in the middle of the night to go break into an abandoned house to steal a non working refrigerator in a stolen car to deliver it to the dope man for thirty dollars only to be told I won't get paid until it was cleaned out! I practically got whip lash turning around to cuss this fool out. "Look

NIGGA this ain't Art Van! Give me my money!" I screamed. He knew I wasn't to be fucked with. He gave me my money and gave Lex some crack.

I grabbed the screw driver to start the van up and politely went to the gas station to get what I needed for Malika. Now this fool Lex gets pissed because he couldn't find a lighter to start smoking immediately and because I wouldn't give him mine. He snatched the remaining money out my hand as if he was going to dog the earnings. Jean looked at me and said, "I know you're not going to let this bitch get away with this shit?" I lost it completely. I pulled away from the gas station at top speed. I drove 90 miles per hour at five in the morning straight down a residential street not yielding or stopping.

Jean looked over at Lex who thought I was playing chicken. Jean told him, "Ain't nobody getting high tonight. Flat out, you gone die bitch." She kept her foot to the pedal not flinching. Now on the corner was a well known Coney Island the neighborhood Police frequented. There were always cops there. Jean didn't give a fuck. She shot across the intersection so fast the van started shaking. Lex shouted, "Stop!!! Stop!!! You crazy bitch!" Jean just laughed and said, "Let's see if you can get high from the grave." A mother in her right mind wouldn't have done that. Not one with a little one at home depending only on her..

It was time for Jean to get me. Her plan was for me to kill myself. She didn't want me dead any other way. It had to be by my own hand. If I committed suicide, she would have been pissed. She wanted me to suffer slowly. She slammed into a park car that was parked kitty corner to our house. We didn't die. The air bags saved us. GOD had his hand on that car.

Lex jumped out running and screaming, "You're a PSYCHO BITCH! You're a crazy bitch!" Jean wasn't anything nice. She got out the van real slow. She was not injured. She was pissed and trying to figure out what went wrong. She wasn't going to be satisfied until I died.

This fool still wouldn't give me my half. I

knew this NIGGA could stomp me without a second thought. What he didn't know was I had been stomped on all my life. Jean retaliated by hitting him with all her might. My cousin shouted at us with her pistol in her hand. We stopped fighting and sat down and smoked the dope. It was totally dysfunctional the way we acted as if nothing had happened. That's how we were living. Drugs can physically take you down but most people don't really take in account of the mental abuse we do to ourselves. Distorted thinking brings fucked up behavior. That brings brain shattering consequences and you continue to lose. No matter how you think you've gotten away with something, you never do. We got ours in the end. Trust me, I am still reaping. Lex eventually went back to jail again. My back wasn't covered. I had to sell my expensive Dautshund, Precious. My jobs became harder because I was alone. It was just me and my little mama.

Phase Nineteen taught me about teamwork.

Phase Twenty

I had been in jail so much. I had not addressed the cases, and ended up having warrants for my arrest again everywhere. I didn't have any money. I was staying with a dear friend, Ant. I call him my brother. I had placed an order for some kitchen cabinets. All I had to do was go get them. I trusted a neighbor with my baby and this bitch took off with Malika. I honestly can't remember her name. She was pregnant and had some issues with her own family at the time. She took Malika to the store while I broke down the cabinets. That decision, like many others, turned out to be a tragedy.

When I went back for them at our meeting place they were gone. I had absolutely no information to locate her. She had no phone number and had just been thrown out of the house she was in that evening. I was devastated. I ran through the streets crying and hollering Malika's name. I felt lost, stupid, scared, and ashamed all at the same time. That's when I made an unselfish decision. I had to call the police. I knew I was going to jail and I would never see her again. That's precisely what happened.

I didn't care. I wanted her found dead or alive. I called the police. Its crazy how your life could just change in a blink of an eye. One minute life is good and in the next breath you're trying to figure out what happened. In the street life anything was bound to happen. You lose one way or another. It's jail or death. On that cold night, October 5, 2006, I lost my life when I lost my last child.

The police picked me up on Meyers and West Chicago. I was taken to the precinct to file for an amber alert. I described my baby's attire to perfection. I did not leave out one detail. Then I proceeded to a jail cell. She was found hours later by Detroit's finest untouched and feisty as ever. I didn't see her again until 2008. My brother Curtis and his wife adopted her. I know she still loves and remembers me. I will always have my regrets for not protecting her all because of my love and obsession for drugs.

When you start using drugs at the age of 16, your brain never really has a chance to finish developing properly. Your brain stops collecting positive data and reverses into a scandalous way of thinking, mine did anyway. I became the devil's side kick at a young age and even though now I have changed, I still have the pain of those memories. I see my children only in the mirrors of the past. I have stalked a couple of them to see how they have grown. I won't say which ones because I would get into trouble for sure. I never speak. I just watch. I know now that the children should have come first.

I don't have my children, but GOD blessed me with a granddaughter, Jamarie's little girl. I keep her five times a week. She has her own room in my house. I have a new chance with her. I'm doing well. She is crazy about her granny. She is truly my heart. Now I know how to take care of a child, just be there, no matter what. GOD will provide you with the help and He does every day.

I was released after that crazy time in my life. I felt sorry for myself. I was alone. I didn't have Lex, my children, a life, a house or a car. It was just me. I asked myself who am I really? Am I really Jean? Does she really exist? Why did she come to me? Better yet, how did she get inside? It's hard to admit that there's more than one person inside of you especially when you know that you have serious problems.

Deep inside you could be hiding a murderer, a rapist, a child molester, or whatever you really are. I know my children will be shocked, some don't care for me. None of them know me or my struggles and pain. I chose to write this book to tell the truth, the whole truth, and nothing but the truth. One day they can read about my life, not all, just enough to get an understanding as to what happened to their real mother. I didn't know how to be a mom. I tried, though some say I didn't try hard enough. I say place your feet near my shoes and I bet you would run. I wear new shoes now. I can't undo what's been etched in stone. I only pray they will one day forgive me and remember I love them.

Once again, I was solo. I was on a serious mission too. The police stopped me in a stolen vehicle with a grenade in the back seat. I was parked at a shopping complex in Dearborn. I was about to commit a major crime. Red was with me. He didn't know my intentions. I asked him to ride with me. Before I was able to complete my well blue printed caper there was a big, black, police issued pistol in my face. An officer shouted, "Do you have the keys to this vehicle?" I instantly held my hands out the window and shouted back, "No sir. This is a stolen car."

Jean was stopped. I was happy about that. The Dearborn Police had us surrounded. I assured them that Red knew nothing about my actions. I was so happy when they let him go. I wasn't worried about the charges. I was relieved to be free from the active addiction, committing crime, and mean spirited adventures of Pamela Jean Marshall. I was definitely going to jail. I had been in and out of jail all my life but this time it was going to be different, I could tell. I ended up in Circuit Court. I was given one of the best Judges in Michigan, Honorable Wade McKree. They called him set 'em free Mckree in the big house.

I had only been in the Wayne County Jail for retail fraud, never anything else. I was charged with receiving and concealing stolen property of a motor vehicle. With my record, I was a little concerned. On the day I was to be sentenced the Judge sent me back for another week so he could think about my sentence. I had never been to prison even though I had eight felony convictions. That was unusual. DAMN!!! I was unusual! Only GOD knows the stress I endured for those seven days wondering what was going to happen to me. Clearly, my luck had run out.

When I returned to court a week later I stood before Judge McKree. He was attractive and nice, but strictly business. He favored no one. He placed you where you were supposed to be based on your record, your behavior, your crime, and his experience. This man was thorough and he didn't play, especially with me. He gave me a choice. He started with a speech I honestly can't remember, all I remember him saying a year in the county or one to five in prison. There was not a doubt in my mind I chose prison. I couldn't do any more county time. County time is the hardest time to do. You can't go anywhere, there are no activities, no yard, well not in Detroit's County Jail. You're stuck in a building breathing recycled air, listening to guards your age telling you what to do. Been there, done that.

I needed something that was going to change my life. He spoke so fast. It was over as soon as it started. I served ten months on my sentence. I can say prison changed my life. I won't go back there. It's easy to get there and hard to get out. I remember quarantine. That was one of the most degrading times in my life. I had to stand in front of this guard completely naked. I was stripped down of everything. All I received at that point was state blues and instructions about how fucked up my stay would be if I didn't follow the rules.

I had two nerve shattering experiences. I was sent to the Robert Scotts Correctional Facility, a woman's prison in Plymouth, Michigan. My first day on the yard there seemed to be a blanket of gloom over the yard. I knew I was in hell. There were three electrical fences to make sure no one got in or out. Some of the women there were in there for unthinkable crimes, the ones you cringe at the thought of. Some of these women had nothing to lose. They were never ever getting out. Some went in doing a year and ended up doing life. I was blessed. I went in and came on home. I was a level one, the lowest non assault level in the prison. I was eligible for the benefits of early release, if I survived. Prison wasn't easy.

The second nerve shattering experience was the Parole Board. See you don't have a date to be released. You have a date for a decision to be made by two out of three people. I came home. One board member asked, "Miss Marshall, what were you going to do with the vehicle, were you going to sell it or commit more crimes with it?" I told the truth.

"If I had not been stopped, I would have committed more crimes. To me, having a car was having money. I couldn't make any without one." I told the board member seriously and humbly that if he gave me a chance to be free, he would never see me again. He then said, "I am going to hold you to that." I was freed on August 7, 2007.

Phase Twenty is when I grew up.

Phase Twenty-One

I have had more dilemmas, but I can honestly say I kept my word. I haven't been back. I am clean and discharged parole on November 6th 2009. I made it. I am winning.

I had the most horrible experiences in my life. I was ready to have a life with GOD. I was so used to having a man as my savior. I finally learned who my personal Savior was and is today. I asked my Father to send me a mate. I prayed for Him to bless me with a man, a good man. Many years later, the Lord gave me a challenge, he sent along a young man name Joshua. All my life I made men my saviors. He was kind of a savior as well. I met him through a mutual friend of my son. He stayed down the street from me. Joshua was very quiet, severely laid back, very hard to read, extremely attractive, 5'10", roughly 175 lbs., and the rarest red golden bronzed skin I have ever seen. Whoo! He had shoulder length hair that he braided to the back, extremely deep dimples, almond brown eyes, and a perfect set of teeth. HE WAS SEXY!! But, here is the kicker, at the time he was 21 years old. Talk about "How Stella Got Her Groove Back!" Joshua brought me back to life. My love for him is magical. Most women will tell you is hard to find. When he is not with me, I miss his touch. He's my baby and I have him on my mind like it's brand new. I'm anxious for him to get home so I can show him how a working man gets treated. He is my true love today. Truthfully, it is scary. Neither one of us wanted to get hurt again. We both have been in some painful relationships. I have learned a lot about painful processes. They can be fixed with real love, hope, and prayer. I prayed for a good man and got one. It didn't matter about the age. Joshua today, is one of my best supporters and dearest friends. I can't imagine being without him and I won't ever give up on true love.

Now that I'm currently serving GOD and loving myself, I can finally love others. This book is not finished. It's only on what I call a stand still. There's more to come. I knew my life was going to be a success somewhere down the line. I just didn't know when. My story is not over.

Pamela Marshall

Pamela Marshall

Order #MPB7192

Order online at
www.mocypublishing.com

for mail orders send money orders to:
Mocy Publishing, LLC
21700 Greenfield, Suite 223
Oak Park, MI 48237

www.ingramcontent.com/pod-product-compliance
Lightning Source LLC
Chambersburg PA
CBHW071310110426
42743CB00042B/1250